Sir James Paget:

Surgeon Extraordinary and his Legacies

Best wishes

Hugh Sturzaker

Published by New Generation Publishing in 2013

Copyright © Hugh Sturzaker 2013

First Edition

The author asserts the moral right under the Copyright, Designs and Patents Act 1988 to be identified as the author of this work.

The illustration on the cover is by permission of the Wellcome Library, London

All Rights reserved. No part of this publication may be reproduced, stored in a retrieval system or transmitted, in any form or by any means without the prior consent of the author, nor be otherwise circulated in any form of binding or cover other than that which it is published and without a similar condition being imposed on the subsequent purchaser.

www.newgeneration-publishing.com

 New Generation **Publishing**

For my family and previous students, trainees and colleagues

CONTENTS

Acknowledgements	6
Prologue	8
Timeline for Sir James Paget	10
1. History of Great Yarmouth	13
2. Parents and Family	25
3. Early years and apprenticeship	35
4. Student life at St. Bartholomew's Hospital	42
5. Lean Period	52
6. Promotions	62
7. Private Practice	71
8. Holidays and Honours	83
9. Retirement from St. Bartholomew's	90
10. Winding down	109
11. Reminiscing	119
12. Old Age	135
Epilogue	141
Main writings of Sir James Paget	180
Synopses of Paget Bicentenary Conference	187
References	216
Index	222

ILLUSTRATIONS

59 South Quay.	13
Samuel Paget.	26
Paget Brewery.	28
Sarah Paget.	30
Sir George Paget.	32
Site of Mr. Bowles School.	36
Woolsey's Mill, near Yarmouth.	37
Front page of 'Natural History of Yarmouth'.	40
St. Bartholomew's quadrangle.	42
Trichina spiralis. Paget's original drawings.	46
Encysted worm in muscle under the microscope.	47
Rahere Ward at St. Barth's 1832.	48
Sir Astley Cooper.	51
Paget lecturing to the students.	57
Hunterian Museum in about 1860.	67
Octavian Dinner Party.	79
James Paget by George Richmond.	84
Portrait of Sir James Paget by John Millais.	92
Sketch of Sir James Paget by Alexander Boswell.	93
Disease of Mammary Areola. First page.	95
Nipple changes in Paget's Disease of Nipple.	96
Group Portrait of College Council 1884-85.	98
Sir James Paget. Chromolithograph by 'Spy'.	102
Paget Disease of Bone. A patient and his hat.	104
Photograph showing bowing of upper right leg.	105
Xray showing thickening of skull bones.	105
Sir James Paget. Photograph in 1881 by G. Jerrard.	110
Sir James Paget Bust by Sir Edgar Boehme.	118
Yarmouth General Hospital on opening day.	126
Florence Nightingale dedication to Sir James.	134
Lady Paget.	136
Sir Julian Paget unveiling bust of Sir James.	164
James Paget University Hospital entrance.	174
Paget's disease of bone. Various illustrations.	211

ACKNOWLEDGEMENTS

The starting point for this book is the 'Memoirs and Letters of Sir James Paget' edited by his son, Stephen, and first published in September 1901 which was less than two years after the death of Sir James. I have used my copy of the book which is the seventh impression which contains additional material and corrections from earlier editions. I have read most of James Paget's books and papers as well as the excellent book 'Sir James Paget: The Rise of Clinical Surgery' by Shirley Roberts published in 1989. Dr. Paul Davies's vast tome 'History of Medicine in Great Yarmouth: Hospitals and Doctors' has given a great insight into doctors and hospitals in Great Yarmouth but also into the history and social life of the town.

It has been very useful to see and study many of the writings and possessions of Sir James in the possession of the Royal College of Surgeons of England and I would like to thank Philippa Mole, Assistant Archivist and Records Manager in the Museums and Archives Department at the College, for all her help and that of her colleagues as well as Sarah Pearson, Curator of the Hunterian Museum at the College.

Sir Julian Paget, great grandson of Sir James, and Sir Julian's son Henry, have been most helpful in talking about Sir James and his family and in providing me with a family tree.

The internet is a rich source of material and information and I have found this invaluable in researching details, not only about Sir James and his family, but also about other people and events mentioned in the book.

For many years I have given talks and lectures about Sir James and most of the illustrations in the book have come from this source and I would like to thank Madeleine Borg, Derek Rogers, Douglas Middleton and Annette Tovell, of the Photographic Department at the James Paget University Hospital, and Carole Reeve, who is Senior Graphic Designer at the hospital, for help in the production of photographs.

I am grateful to Christine Thompson and her successor, Peter Ransome, Librarians of the Sir James Paget Library at the hospital for their help.

I would like to thank the Royal College of Surgeons, the Wellcome Trust, St. Bartholomew's Hospital, James Paget University Hospital and Sir Julian Paget for permission to include in this book photographs and images in their possession.

I have managed to obtain synopses from most of the speakers at the Paget Bicentenary Conference for inclusion in the book. All are extremely busy people but at least meeting the deadline for the publication of the book has enabled them to focus on and prepare for the talks they are going to give in January. I am grateful to Mark Wilkinson, Professor Harold Ellis, Professor Ian Mcmanus, Professor David Crossman, Professor Jerome Pereira, Dick Rainsbury, Sue Down, Karen Flores, Professor Bill Fraser, Professor Simon Donell, Willy Notcutt and Sir Julian Paget.

Daniel Cooke and Sam Rennie of New Generation Publishing have been wonderfully supporting with their advice and patience in getting this book to print and I am most grateful to them.

I would like to thank David Wright and Christine Allen, Chairman and Chief Executive respectively, of the James Paget University Hospitals NHS Foundation Trust for supporting the Paget Bicentenary Celebrations and for making the Conference possible.

If I have forgotten to mention anyone in these acknowledgements please forgive me.

Finally, I would like to thank Ann, my wife, for her forbearance, patience and for being a great supplier of drinks and refreshments.

PROLOGUE

Saturday 11 January 2014 is the two-hundredth anniversary of the birth of James Paget in Great Yarmouth, Norfolk and, to mark that occasion, a number of celebrations are planned. There will be an all day conference in the hospital named after him - The James Paget University Hospital -, a dinner in Great Yarmouth Town Hall, a civic service in Great Yarmouth Minster led by the Bishop of Norwich on the Sunday, exhibitions in the Minster and the hospital about his life and the unveiling of a plaque at the site where he was born. The Royal College of Surgeons of England is also staging an exhibition about him. In addition, this book is being published.

Why write a book about a man who was born two hundred years ago? Is there anything to be gained by doing so? He was born into a wealthy family in a prosperous Georgian seaside port and for the first ten years of his life led an idyllic childhood. Then his businessman father started getting into financial difficulties and we see the effects that this had on the whole family. In spite of this - and to a certain extent perhaps because of it - James went on to become one of the leading and most respected surgeons of his time. Not only was he a good surgeon, he was a superb clinician, a great teacher, writer and orator and he is regarded as the father of British Pathology. He was surgeon to Queen Victoria and the Prince of Wales, President of the Royal College of Surgeons of England, Vice Chancellor of London University and president or chairman of numerous societies, commissions and committees. He was a Fellow of the Royal Society, and had honours bestowed on him from universities and institutions from all over the world.

James Paget is probably best known for two diseases named after him: Paget's Disease of Bone and Paget's disease of the Nipple, but he is credited with describing ten conditions which had not been appreciated before.

He was very much a family man who, with his wife Lydia, led by example and instruction of his six children. One became a successful barrister and writer, two became bishops and the fourth son became a surgeon and, later, a much more successful writer. James was deeply religious, kind, courteous and was almost worshipped by his students, patients and hospital staff. He was friends with all the most distinguished scientists and medical people of the day as well as with the artists, writers and politicians. He was feted by high society.

This book is a chronological history of his life and starts by tracing the history of Great Yarmouth where he was born. At the end I have tried to analyse the reasons for his success and the legacies that he has left behind.

Undoubtably, he benefitted from some good genes and a stable family life as his older brother, Sir George Paget, was Regius Professor of Physic at Cambridge University, President of the General Medical Council, a Fellow of the Royal Society and an extremely good physician and teacher. However, James's true success came from his great powers of observation, his ability at 'orderly arrangement' and his work ethic. As he said 'Work itself is a pleasure..... there is no success without it, no happiness without it.' There is much that we can learn from Sir James and I hope you enjoy and benefit from reading this book.

Timeline for Sir James Paget

1814 January 11	Born in Great Yarmouth
1830 March 9	Starts Apprenticeship with Dr. Costerton
1834	Publication of 'Sketch of the Natural History of Great Yarmouth and its Neighbourhood'.
October	Medical student at St. Bartholomew's Hospital
1835 February 2	Discovers Trichina spiralis
1836 May 13	Passed the Membership Examination of the Royal College of Surgeons
	Becomes engaged to Lydia North
1837	Curator of St. Bartholomew's Hospital Museum
1839	Demonstratorship of Morbid Anatomy at St. Bartholomew's
1841 April 14	Elected Surgeon to the Finsbury Dispensary
1842	Appointed to catalogue specimens in Hunterian Museum of Royal College of Surgeons
1843 May 30	Appointed Lecturer in Physiology at St. Bartholomew's
August 8	Appointed first warden of College for St. Bartholomew's medical students
November	Elected Foundation Fellow of Royal College of Surgeons of England. One of 300 and the youngest
1844 May	Married Lydia North
1847 January	Appointed Professor of Anatomy and Surgery at Royal College of Surgeons to give Arris and Gale Lectures
1847 February	Elected Assistant Surgeon at St. Bartholomew's
1848	Publication of Kirke's Handbook of Physiology
1849	Completed the Pathological Catalogue of the College of Surgeons' Museum
1851	Took on private surgical practice more or less full time
	Elected to Fellowship of the Royal Society
1852	Moved to 24 Henrietta Street, Cavendish Square
1853	Publication of 'Lectures in Surgical Pathology'
1854	Appointed examiner to the East India Company
1857	Croonian Lecture 'On the Cause of the Rhythmic Motion of the Heart'
1858 January	Moved to 1 Harewood Place, Hanover Square
March	Appointed Surgeon Extraordinary to Queen Victoria
1859 April 8	Lecture at Royal Institution on 'The Chronometry of Life'
June 14	Resigns as Lecturer in Physiology
1860	Joined Senate of London University

1861 July 24	Appointed Surgeon of St. Bartholomew's
1862	Paid final instalment of his father's debts
January 23	Appointed Surgeon to Christ's Hospital
	Address to British Medical Association 'On treatment of patients after surgical operations'.
1863	Appointed Surgeon-in-Ordinary to the Prince of Wales
October 1	Introductory Address to medical students at St. Bartholomew's
1865 July	Elected to Council of the Royal College of Surgeons
	Appointed Joint Lecturer in Surgery at St. Bartholomew's with Mr. Holmes Coote
1869 April	Appointed a member of the Royal Sanitary Commission
	President of Clinical Society of London
	Published 'What becomes of Medical Students?' in St. Bartholomew's Reports
1871	Resigned as Surgeon from St. Bartholomew's and appointed Consulting Surgeon
	Appointed a baronet
1872	Elected Fellow of Linnean Society
1873	Portrait painted by John Millais presented by his colleagues and friends
1874	President of Section of Surgery of British Medical Association in Norwich
	Paper 'On Disease of the Mammary Areola Preceding Cancer of the Mammary Gland' in St. Bartholomew's Hospital Report
1875	Elected President of Royal College of Surgeons of England
	President of the Royal Medico-Chirurgical Society
	Publication of 'Clinical Lectures and Essays'
1876	Publication in 'Vanity Fair' of Spy's caricature of him
1876 July 13	Appointed to General Medical Council
November 14	Paper 'On a form of chronic inflammation of the bones (osteitis deformans)' presented to Medico-Chirurgical Society
1877 February 13	Hunterian Oration of Royal College of Surgeons of England Stopped operating except on small cases
1880 August	President of Section of Pathology at British Medical Association meeting in Cambridge. Lectured on 'Elemental Pathology'
1881 February 10	Appointed Governor of St. Bartholomew's Hospital

	August	President of Seventh International Medical Congress
	November	Appointed to the Hospital's Commission
	November 11	Elected Honorary Fellow of Medical Society of London
1882	December 13	Gave first Bradshawe Lecture at Royal College of Surgeons 'On some Rare and New Diseases'
1883	April	Elected Vice-Chancellor of London University
1884	June	Appointed Vice-President of International Health Exhibition
1885	March 23	Elected Corresponding Member of the Académie des Sciences
	August 6	Royal College of Surgeons commissioned Sir Edgar Boehme to produce a bust of him
1885		Publication of the new edition of the Pathological Catalogue of the Museum of the Royal College of Surgeons
	June 8	Talk to Abernethian Society of St. Bartholomew's on 'St.Bartholomew's Hospital and School fifty years ago'
1886		Finished writing his memoirs
	April	Appointed Chairman of Pasteur Committee
1887		President of Pathological Society of London
1888	September 20	Opened Great Yarmouth General Hospital
1889	May	Appointed to Royal Commission on Vaccination
1891		'Studies of Old Case-Books' published
		Chairman of Virchow Testimonial Fund to celebrate Virchow's Seventieth birthday
1893	September	Moved to 5 Park Square West Regent's Park
1894		Last address to students given at Abernethian Society
1895	January 7	Lydia, his wife, dies
		St. Bartholomew's names a ward after him
1897	April	Royal College of Surgeons awarded him the Honorary Gold Medal of the College
1899	December 30	Dies peacefully at his home
1900	January 4	Funeral in Westminster Abbey

1

HISTORY OF GREAT YARMOUTH

James Paget was born at 4 p.m. on 11 January 1814 in a mansion on South Quay in Great Yarmouth, Norfolk. His father Samuel was a prosperous merchant and had completed the building of the house on the site of his original one the previous year. Yet, within ten years, Samuel's businesses were failing and James was unable to attend Charterhouse School in London where his elder brothers had been educated. Nevertheless, James went on to become one of the leading and most respected surgeons of his day. To understand how this was achieved we need to look at Great Yarmouth in the early part of the nineteenth century and at his parents and siblings before tracing his life. His story illustrates what can be achieved by determination and hard work.

59 South Quay
(Great Yarmouth Borough Council)

Great Yarmouth is built on a sandbank which developed in the mouth of a large estuary opening into the North Sea. The estuary was fed by the rivers Bure, Yare and Waveney and its mouth extended eight miles from the present day Caister-on-Sea in the north to Corton in the south. The Romans first came to the area in 46AD and started building a Roman encampment in 100 AD at Burgh Castle on the south side of the estuary and they built another one, 150 years later, on the north side at what is now known as Caister. These forts were manned by the Roman army and navy to defend the lands they had captured and then farmed from the invading Saxons

Over the years the passageway north of the sandbank, known as Cocklewater or Grubb's Haven, started to silt up so that by 1066 the sandbank was connected to the mainland. For many centuries the sandbank had been used as a base for fisherman catching the plentiful supply of fish off the coast. Gradually homesteads started to be built and small communities were based around the highest part of the land which is now known as Fuller's Hill. In 495 Cerdic, a Saxon Prince and his son, Cenrick attacked this settlement and burnt it to the ground. St. Bennet's Church had been built in this area at the time of Edward the Confessor but it was pulled down about the time that Bishop Hebert de Lozinga, first Bishop of Norwich, founded St Nicholas Church in 1101. The church was consecrated in 1119 and subsequently enlarged in 1123, 1250 and 1381 to become the largest parish church in the country. It was firebombed in the early hours of 25 June 1942 by German bombers. Only the tower and the walls remained but it was rebuilt in the 1950s and reconsecrated on 8 May 1961.

Yarmouth's fortunes were built on the fishing industry, especially the herring, and its proximity to Holland enabled it to become a prosperous port for the import and export of goods between England and the continent. Long before houses were built on the sandbank people used to fish from it and each October and November there was a prolific supply of herring. The herring had the advantage of being plentiful and it could be preserved in salt enabling it to be transported all over the country in barrels. Later it was exported widely to Europe e.g. Naples, Venice, Genoa, Ancona, Trieste, Bordeaux and Russia.

The herring catch varied from year to year but, for many years, Yarmouth was the herring capital of the world. The importance of the herring and its royal recognition resulted in Edward III granting a coat of arms to the town in 1340 in which the three royal lions occupy the left hand of the shield and the tails of three herrings occupy the right side.

Another means of preserving the fish was by smoking to produce kippers and Yarmouth had many smoke houses for this purpose. It also produced its own version known as a bloater. In both cases the herring is salted in brine before smoking. The kipper is opened up longitudinally before smoking whereas the bloater is smoked whole without gutting.

A continuing problem for the port was the recurrent silting up of the remaining river channel which passed west and south of the peninsular of sand on which Yarmouth was developing. Various attempts were made to overcome this by digging out new channels or havens and the first one was cut in 1346. In 1393 a second one was required and a third in 1408. The fourth haven was made in 1508 and another in 1529. Twenty years later another was needed and this was paid for by selling off the church's plate, ornaments and robes as well as the steeple bells. This raised £1816.9s.7d and the task required 100 men working each day. Even this haven started to silt up and eventually a Dutchman was employed to tackle the problem. He constructed an outlet into the sea at right angles to the coast so that the speed of the river flow would prevent it from silting up. Work was started on 8 January 1560 with nearly 1000 men and was completed on 4 March. The concept was so successful that it is still functioning.

Because of the repeated silting up of the river the port was not always usable, so a jetty was built from the beach out into the sea in 1560. This enabled fish to be landed, for ships to be loaded and unloaded and for larger vessels, at anchor offshore in the shelter of the Scroby sands (another sandbank), to be serviced. There was a crane at the eastern end of the jetty to help load and unload vessels but the jetty was at the mercy of the sea and winds. It was rebuilt in 1701 but in 1767 about 100 feet of it were swept away and more in 1791. Most of it was destroyed by a storm in 1805 but was rebuilt four years later and lengthened in 1846 and 1870. In recent years the width of the beach at Yarmouth has grown, so that much of the jetty was surrounded by sand and only the end was in the sea. For safety reasons, access to the jetty was prevented and, after English Heritage failed to support its renovation, it was removed in 2011. A plaque now records its history.

On 12 March 1801 Vice Admiral Lord Nelson left from the jetty to join the Grand Fleet of 47 ships under the command of Admiral Sir Hyde Parker before the Battle of Copenhagen on the 2 April 1801. Following this great victory he returned to Great Yarmouth and landed at the jetty from the gun-brig Kite on July 1 to visit the wounded men in the Hospital for Sick and Wounded of the Army and Navy.

Nelson had visited Yarmouth previously in 1800, two years after he destroyed the French Fleet at the battle of the Nile. Following that battle he had stayed with the British Ambassador Sir William Hamilton and his wife, Emma, in Naples for nearly two years before he was ordered home. The three then travelled across Europe and sailed from Cuxhaven in the mail packet King George, eventually landing south of the river at Gorleston on 6 November 1800. There the party was received by the Mayor and other officials before continuing along the south bank of the river to the Haven Bridge. Here the horses were detached from Nelson's coach and it was pulled across the bridge and into the town by many of the local people. The visitors were taken to the main hostelry, The Wrestlers' Inn, just off the Market Place and shortly afterward Nelson appeared at a window and said "I am myself a Norfolk man and I glory in being so." He then attended a reception at which he was presented with the freedom of the Borough during which he was asked for his right hand to take the oath. He replied "That is in Tenerife." The next day he attended a service in St. Nicholas Church and before leaving Yarmouth he gave the Mayor £50 for "the necessitous poor of the town".

Nelson left for London on 8 November escorted out of the town by Captain Lacon. Before leaving Nelson was asked by Mrs. Suckling, the landlady of the Wrestlers' Inn, if it could be renamed "The Nelson Arms." He replied "That would be absurd seeing that I only have one." The inn was subsequently

named The Nelson Hotel but by 1836 it was again named The Wrestlers' Inn.
   Sadly Nelson was killed at the Battle of Trafalgar in 1805. In spite of his affair with Lady Hamilton he was regarded as a national hero and on 11 August 1814, it was proposed to start a subscription to erect a memorial to him in Norfolk. Nearly £7,000 were raised and it was decided to erect a column on the sandy Denes, south of Yarmouth in the centre of the recently established officers' racecourse. The first stone was laid by Colonel Wodehouse on 15 August 1817 and the work was completed in 1819. The column is 144 feet high with 217 steps within it. It is built of brick and faced with quartz sandstone from quarries at Cullalloe in Fife, Scotland. On top stands the figure of Britannia with arms outstretched. There was some consternation that Britannia was not facing the sea until it was pointed out that she was looking towards Burnham Thorpe where Nelson was born in 1758.
   A priory was built next to St. Nicholas Church and a monastery of Black Friars was founded by St. Dominica in 1204 in the southern part of the town. In 1279 the Whitefriars or Carmelites founded a monastery further north but his was destroyed by fire in 1509. In 1525 the Church of the Dominicans was burnt down.
   With its increasing wealth there was always the fear of attack, so in 1261 Henry III granted licences for fortifying the town and on 12 September 1262 he granted a charter for enclosing the town with a wall and a moat. This work was carried out by those living in the town, although the wealthy could pay for others to do their share of the work. The construction was mainly from flints picked up from the beach and surrounding area as well as some brick. In 1396, after 111 years, the fortifications were completed and the town could boast of having a wall 2,280 yards long with 20 towers and 10 gates. The town was surrounded on its north, east and south sides by the wall and on its west side by the river. The height of the wall was 23 feet and when war against France was declared in 1545 the wall was strengthened by piling a rampart of sand and earth against the inside of the wall. For many centuries no building was allowed outside the walls so the inhabitants would

look out on the sand dunes and sea. The dunes were used by the fisherman to dry and repair their nets.

By the 1300s many naval ships were using the port of Yarmouth and its importance as a naval port grew over the years. Many ships could berth in the long stretch of river between the long sandy peninsular on which Yarmouth was built and the opposite bank. They were protected from the rough seas and winds and invaders could be prevented from entering the river by putting a boom or chain across the mouth of the river. The other attraction to the navy was that larger vessels could anchor off the coast where they received some protection from the many sandbanks which had developed east of the town.

Entrance to the town was mainly from the North through the northgate although there was a ferry across the river for horses, carts, cattle and foot passengers. In 1427 a bridge was built across the river which was replaced by drawbridges in 1553, 1570, 1785 and 1886.

The central part of the town was the Market Place, just south of St Nicholas Church. It was in the Market Place that people met and bought and sold produce and in 1384 it was paved and a market cross and Pillory built. The butchers were on the east side of the Market Place with their slaughter houses and unused parts tended to be thrown over the town wall. It is thought that a castle was built in the centre of the town in 1330 but this was demolished in 1621.

Houses were built along narrow alleyways called "rows" which ran in a west-east direction from the river. The rows were first mentioned in 1198 and developed over the next 100 years. Eventually there were 145 rows, being numbered from the north southwards. They were so narrow that it was possible for people to reach out from a window and touch people opposite. Doors to houses used to open outwards but this caused obstructions so a law was issued requiring all doors to open inwards. To transport goods and possessions through the narrow rows the Yarmouth Troll Cart evolved. It had four wheels which were under the carriage. It was also called the Yarmouth Coach. Sanitation was poor and people threw their waste and dirty water into the rows. It was not surprising that the plague hit the town and its inhabitants on several occasions.

In 1334 only York, Bristol and London raised more taxes than Yarmouth and in 1348 there were 220 boats in the river. The Plague (Black Death) struck in 1349 when two-thirds of the population died and it was many years before the community was able to recover and become wealthy again. In 1561 three town wells were opened to provide fresh water. From May to September 1579 there was another outbreak of plague and 2000 people died.

In spite of the population being devastated by the Plague Yarmouth continued to grow and increase in prosperity due to its successful fishing industry and being a thriving port. The herring, in particular, was the mainstay of its success and it was preserved in salt and by smoking and was exported to many countries in Europe and beyond. The Yarmouth Bloater became very popular and this was a herring which was smoked intact rather than being opened up like a kipper.

Servicing of the naval fleet was important and helped to finance the town's success. Press gangs were also active in the town to obtain sailors for the naval ships. The dangers of the sea were never far away and many ships were destroyed along the coast and it was not uncommon to find the bodies of the ships' crew washed up on the beach.

The importance of Yarmouth was also recognised by the many members of Royalty that visited and passed through the port. It's royal connections go back to 1041 when Yarmouth belonged to Edward the Confessor and it was run by 70 burgesses. King John granted it its first charter in 1209. In 1257 Henry III granted the town certain franchises and in 1262 granted a charter to enclose the town with a wall and a moat. In 1342 Edward III joined the Yarmouth squadron for his expedition to Brittany. Forty years later, in 1382, Richard II visited the town and stayed in the great hall of the priory attached to St. Nicholas Church. In 1403 Henry VI granted by consent of Parliament that the shipping, weighing and packing of wool, hides and skins should be done in Yarmouth as it was a frontier town.

Charles II visited the town in 1671. Several years previously the town had supported the Parliamentarian's cause and in 1648 a group of local men signed a document at 4 South Quay which led to the execution of Charles I on 30 January 1649. In 1692 William III landed at Yarmouth. Louise XVIII came in 1807 and the Prince of Orange in 1813.

With their increasing wealth, merchants started to knock down the houses at the western end of the rows and build large mansions facing South Quay. This gave them good views across the river and enabled them to keep an eye on their ships and staff. Many of these houses were built in the seventeenth and eighteenth century although 59 South Quay, built by James Paget's father, was completed in 1813 on the site of his previous house. A columned town hall was built at the northern end of South Quay in 1716. The whole of this quay was one of wealth and affluence and this is recorded by Daniel Defoe in 1724 in his book "A tour thro' the whole island of Great Britain, divided into circuits or journies." He wrote: "Yarmouth is an antient town, much older than Norwich; and at present, tho' not standing on so much ground, yet better built; much more compleat; for number of inhabitants, not much inferior; and for wealth trade and advantage of its situation, infinitely superior to Norwich...... and the town facing to the West also, and open to the river, makes the finest key in England, if not in Europe, not inferior even to that of Marseilles itself." He goes on to say that the ships are so close along the quay. " In this pleasant and agreeable range of houses are some very magnificent buildings, and among the rest, the custom-house and town hall, and some merchants houses, which look like little palaces, rather than the dwelling-houses of private men."

In spite of the visible wealth of South Quay and in other parts of the town there was severe poverty for the people living in the rows. There was poor nutrition and infectious diseases were common. Many babies died and the lives of adults were cut short by a combination of accidents at work and infectious diseases.

Medical care in the seventeenth and eighteenth century was rudimentary. There were few effective drugs but many applications were made from plants and some minerals. There were no anaesthetics and causes of infection were unknown. Abscesses were drained with a scalpel and all manner of conditions were treated by bleeding, usually by piercing a vein in the arm and allowing the blood to flow until the patient felt faint. Leeches were also used to remove blood. An injured limb was usually treated by its removal and only about half of the patients survived. A similar mortality was found in patients who were subjected to cutting for a stone in their bladder. They died from a combination of infection and blood loss.

There had been hospitals in Yarmouth since the 13th century when Thomas Fastolph founded one dedicated to the Virgin Mary. It was to house the poor and destitute and occupied an area on the east side of the Market Place extending to the Pudding Gate. The wealthier people were treated in their own homes. In 1538, at the Dissolution of the Monasteries, the hospital was closed and the care of the poor was transferred from the church to the local authorities.

Eventually, in 1597 the local authority decided to build onto the south side of St. Mary's a house of correction for the poor, similar to the Bridewell in London. This was a place where the poor and destitute could receive shelter and food in exchange for carrying out menial tasks and was the forerunner of the workhouse. Eden's survey of the poor in England in 1797 said that the poor were mainly maintained in a Poorhouse where they were employed in making nets for mackerel and other small fish. There were separate rooms for men, women, boys and girls and there were 15-16 beds to a room. Married couple were given a separate room and there were two rooms for the sick. Housed here were 65 men, 148 women, 40 boys and 42 girls. By 1836 the workhouse was occupied by three to four hundred people. In addition there were 78 poor houses which were occupied by poor families rent free. A new workhouse was built outside the town walls to the east of Northgate Street in 1838. With the coming of the National Health Service in 1948 it became Northgate Hospital looking after medical patients and later having a maternity unit built in its grounds.

The Fisherman's Hospital was built by Yarmouth Corporation on the east side of the Market Place in 1702 to house 20 fisherman and their wives who were poor and over the age of 60 years. In spite of its name it was not to treat the sick but to provide accommodation for poor fisherman. They were also given a small sum of money each week and some coal in the winter.

In 1793 a hospital for wounded sailors and soldiers was built next to a distillery outside the town walls, east of the moat on St. Nicholas Road. Two years later the grounds of the distillery were acquired by the government to build a barracks to hold 1,600 men and the hospital was enclosed within the grounds of the barracks. John Bell was one of the people looking after the wounded in this hospital and decried the poor training that naval surgeons received. He wrote extensively on how the wounded could be better treated and published " Discourse on the Nature and Cure of Wounds" and a "Memoir Concerning the Present State of Military and Naval Surgery".

In 1797 the British fleet set sail from Yarmouth to attack the Dutch fleet at the Battle of Camperdown. They were victorious but 1,040 were killed or injured. The wounded were brought back to Yarmouth and taken to the barrack hospital, with the more seriously wounded being taken to Norwich. Many died from infection and gangrene. In 1801, after the Battle of Copenhagen, the injured were taken to the barrack hospital and Nelson visited and spoke to each patient.

Apart from the military and naval hospitals for treating the wounded there were few hospitals for treating the sick outside London. The Norfolk and Norwich Hospital was built in 1771 and a Dispensary for treating the sick poor was opened in Queen Street, Yarmouth in 1826. Initially it treated the poor and sick as outpatients but by 1838 it was able to provide 3-4 beds so that patients could be admitted for treatment. Five honorary medical officers were appointed - two physicians and three surgeons - and among the latter was Dr. Charles Costerton who was the Paget family doctor. The facilities in the Dispensary were soon inadequate and in 1840, having raised money by public subscription, a new hospital was built on the mount immediately outside the town wall east of St. George's Chapel. Initially there were 12 beds but this was increased to 20 by moving them closer together.

Beer was a standard drink for most people as in many instances water was often polluted. To meet this demand there were several breweries in the town and many taverns. In 1555 brewing was only allowed with the permission of the bailiffs and in 1572 coal had to be used to brew rather than wood and every ale house had to be licensed by the bailiffs. In 1637 there were thirty-four brewing houses in the town. From the eighteenth century onwards the leading brewery was Lacon's and in 1804 an established brewery on North Quay opposite the Conge was bought by Samuel Paget and Company. The population of the town in 1801 was 14,854.

Thus, by the time of James Paget's birth, Great Yarmouth was a prosperous Georgian town and seaport. Its main source of wealth came from the sea in the large catches of fish - especially the herring in October and November - but also in the export of goods from East Anglia, such as corn and cotton goods, and the import of goods from the continent. Iron, pitch and wood came from Russia, Sweden and Norway. Yarmouth was also a prominent naval port for fighting the French, Dutch and Spaniards and had provided medical care for those injured in the battles.

The wealth of the town was clearly visible along the impressive South Quay where large merchant houses stood side by side. One of the prominent members of the community was Dawson Turner who was a wealthy banker, botanist and a supporter of the arts. He lived in a large house on Hall Quay facing the bridge which brought traffic over the river into Yarmouth. The bank's activities were conducted on the ground floor while he and his family lived on the floors above. One of his partners was Samuel Paget, James' father, and Dawson Turner was to play a significant part in putting James in contact with some of the leading scientists of the day.

However, there was much poverty where many people were crammed into substandard housing in the rows. There was no sanitation and dirty water was thrown onto the rows. Infectious diseases were therefore common and life expectancy was low. The town did provide accommodation and spartan food for the poor in exchange for performing menial tasks. Towards the end of the eighteenth century a hospital was built to tend to the sailors injured in battle and, in the early part of the nineteenth century, a dispensary was established for treating the poor as outpatients.

This was the place where James was born and grew up. He would have seen the contrasts between the wealth on South Quay and the poverty in the rows. He would have had the opportunity of playing on the sand dunes, walking in the surrounding countryside and visiting the small towns and villages of Gorleston, Caister, Bradwell, Corton, and Burgh Castle. He would witness the fishermen unloading their catches and would converse with the captains and seamen of his father's boats which brought back produce from many foreign lands. He would admire the naval officers, in their splendid uniforms, walking up and down the quay. He would visit his father's brewery and he and his brothers would sketch many of the local sights. The town was confined by the town wall and the river and was only just beginning to expand beyond the walls. He would know all parts of it well and each Sunday would accompany his parents to St. Nicholas Church for the services. The church's cemetery was where many of his young brothers and sisters had been buried. Disease and early death were common and he experienced this in his own family.

2

PARENTS AND FAMILY

Samuel Paget, James's father, was born on 1 December 1774 of humble origins but went on to become a successful businessman. James remembers him as "a good cricketer, a good speaker, gentle, calm, busy all day, and always seeming to love more than anything the quiet of his home." On 1 December 1896 James said of him that he "was a thoroughly good man, a gentleman in his very nature, only too hopeful, and too generous even to his children." Samuel's father was said to be "an idle and rather dissolute man, from whom he derived no money or help in either teaching or example." His mother, on the other hand, was "prudent, gentle, affectionate, helpful even in the business of his early life."

Samuel Paget
(Sir Julian Paget)

Samuel's education was rudimentary enabling him to read, write and do some arithmetic but he went on to become one of the best letter writers that James ever knew. On leaving school he became clerk to Mr. Kerridge, a local merchant who provided the naval ships with provisions. Mr Kerridge died unexpectedly when Samuel was 17 in 1791 and Samuel decided to go to London to try to obtain the contract with the Royal Navy that Mr. Kerridge had previously had. The journey took nearly 24 hours and Samuel was amazed at the size of London. Somehow he convinced the Admiralty that he should take over Mr. Kerridge's contract and with the help of his mother he was able to borrow money to finance the business.

Through hard work he became a very successful businessman. He was punctual and his colleagues considered him fair, liberal and honest. Lord Duncan praised him publicly in 1779 after the battle of Camperdown for he had managed to supply the fleet moored in Yarmouth Roads (The water between the coast and the sandbanks offshore which gave some protection from the North Sea) with supplies in extremely short time. After the victory the town gave a celebratory dinner and drank Lord Duncan's health but he pointed to Samuel saying "That's the man that won the battle" and later gave him a gold medal engraved "Earl St. Vincent's testimony of Approbation".

In November 1800, when Lord Nelson visited Yarmouth, following his earlier victory at the battle of the Nile, the Mayor of Yarmouth and Captain Samuel Paget, each of whom commanded a Volunteer Corps, marched with their band to the Wrestlers' Inn where Lord Nelson was staying and fired three volleys in his honour.

As his business became more successful he took on other ventures such as a brewery, which eventually had over twenty-five inns; he was the owner of several ships and a partner in a bank with Dawson Turner. Dawson Turner (1775-1858) was the grandson of the Reverend Francis Turner who had four sons: Francis was an apothecary and surgeon in Yarmouth; Richard was master of Yarmouth Grammar school; James was Mayor of Yarmouth in 1779 and a founder of Gurney's Bank and Joseph was Master of Pembroke Hall, Cambridge, Dean of Norwich Cathedral and a friend of William Pitt. Dawson Turner joined the bank established by his father James Turner and, when it moved to Hall Quay, he and his family lived above the bank. Dawson was a famous naturalist, writer and supporter of artists. Years later the bank was taken over by Barclays and still stands on Hall Quay today.

Paget Brewery. Pencil Sketch by Charles Paget
(Sir Julian Paget)

Samuel Paget became senior partner in the brewery in 1804 when it was bought from another firm. It became known as Paget and Company and supplied fifty-four public houses in Yarmouth and several outside the town. It was built in North Quay and was the second largest brewery in town; the biggest being owned by Sir Edmund Lacon. Initially it was a profitable enterprise for the young Samuel Paget but unfortunately, this would not continue.

Samuel Paget was a very active and public spirited man and was mayor of Yarmouth in 1817. He was the leader and lieutenant-colonel of a volunteer corps raised at the time of Napoleon's threatened invasion. He was also involved in many charities in the town.

With his wealth he bought many books and acquired a great library for the benefit of his children. Among his botanical books were the great "English Botany; or coloured figures of British plants" (1790-1814) of Sir James Smith and James Sowerby in 36 volumes with 2,592 coloured plates of all known Phanerogams (A plant which produces seeds) and Dawson Turner's beautifully illustrated book on seaweeds which James knew as the "Historia Fucorum" (1808-1819).

However, from the early 1820s Samuel Paget was getting into financial difficulties because of failures in some of his businesses and the fact that the navy was withdrawing from the port as the threat from the French had disappeared. His situation was made worse by the crippling interest charges he was having to pay to his friend and business colleague Dawson Turner. Dr. Mark Rumble, a retired general practitioner, records in his history of Yarmouth that in "the deeds of no. 68 King Street, I found details of Paget's business, and details of the mortgage that he held with Dawson Turner. Business however went into a steep decline, and in 1831 Paget was paying Gurney, Turner and Brightwen the sum of £6,000 per annum in interest upon a loan of £60,000 with all of Paget's properties mortgaged to them." Clearly this was unsustainable and led to Paget's impoverishment which was only mitigated by his sons agreeing to pay off his debts over many years.

In 1799, at the age of 25, Samuel married Sarah Elizabeth Tolver. She had been much better educated. Her father, Tom Tolver, had married a rich widow and together they had three daughters. It seems that he never had the need to work and when his wife died he had further financial support from an old lady who lived with him and his two younger daughters. James's mother was adopted as a child by Tom Tolver's sister, Mrs. Godfrey who was the wife of a rich Yarmouth man. James describes his mother as "handsome, tall and graceful, somewhat hasty in temper, resolute, strong-willed and strong in speech. However, the qualities which one best remembers were her intense love of her children, her marvellous activity and industry, her admiration of all that was beautiful in art and nature, her skill in writing, needlework and painting."

Sarah Paget
(Sir Julian Paget)

She was instrumental in overseeing the upbringing of her children as well as the running of the home. She was also a great collector of autographs, seals and caricatures, shells, corals and agates, old china and glass and curiosities of all kinds. She induced the masters of her husband's ships to bring back objects to add to her collections. All of them were orderly arranged and labelled. She was an enthusiastic painter and had lessons by John Chrome (1768-1821) who was born in Norwich and was the founder of the Norwich School of painters. He worked in watercolour and oil and visited her home weekly to teach her and her children.

She was involved in many charities in the town and played an active part in politics supporting the Tory party.

Sarah started giving birth to babies almost annually from

1800 and her youngest daughter was born in 1825. Four of her first seven children did not live beyond their first year and another two died at the ages of four and six. Common causes of death then were diphtheria, measles and scarlet fever. Of their seventeen children born over twenty-five years only nine reached adult hood and of these Arthur died aged 25, Charles aged 33 and Francis at the age of 32. The remaining six survived as follows: Martha to 81 years, Frederick to 62 years, George to 81, James to 85, Alfred to 44, and Katherine to 60.

A complete list of the family is as follows:

Martha Maud Paget (Patty) (1800-1881) did not marry.

Samuel Paget (1801-1801) died less than 2 months old.

Samuel Paget (1802-1808)Died aged 4.

Thomas Paget (1803-1803).

Henry Thomas Paget (1804-1808).

Frederick Paget (1805-1867) He went to Charterhouse School and later emigrated to Vienna and went into business. He married and had 7 sons and 2 daughters.

Elizabeth Sarah Paget (1807-1808).

Arthur Coyte Paget (1808-1833 December 26). After schooling at Charterhouse he went to Cambridge but spent most of his time socialising and neglecting his studies. In 1831 he entered Chambers at the Temple. He lived in shabby lodgings and fell in love but his advances were turned down. He was friends with William Makepeace Thackeray (1811-1863), the novelist who also went to Charterhouse and Cambridge. Both of them were idle as students and after they left Cambridge but Thackeray was a changed man by his marriage in 1836 and began to write seriously. In 1833 Arthur became ill and his father brought him back to Yarmouth. He became very moody and the only person he would allow to look after him was

James. He died from consumption aged 25 on December 26 1833.

George Edward Paget (1809-1892), along with James was the most successful of the brothers.

Sir George Paget
(Sir Julian Paget)

After Charterhouse, where he won prizes in mathematics, he went to Gonville and Caius College, Cambridge. He did very well in Mathematics in 1831 and in 1832 was awarded a

Fellowship at Caius College. The condition of the fellowship was that it went to a Norfolk man to study Medicine. He studied physic, anatomy and chemistry at Cambridge and St. Bartholomew's, obtaining his Doctorate of Medicine in 1838. He became a Fellow of the Royal College of Physicians in 1839 and was appointed physician to Addenbrooke's Hospital in 1839 at the age of 29. In 1856 he was elected to the Council of the University Senate. He was the University's representative on the General Medical Council from 1863 and elected its President in 1869, serving until 1874. He was President of the British Medical Association in1864 and was Regius Professor of Physic at Cambridge from 1872 until his death in 1892. He and Sir George Humphrey, the Professor of Surgery, are regarded as re-vitalising the School of Medicine in Cambridge. He was elected a Fellow of the Royal Society in 1873 and knighted in 1878. He had recurrent attacks of rheumatic fever throughout his life. He married Clara Fardell at the age of 41 in 1851 and they had five sons and five daughters with seven surviving to adulthood.

Charles John Paget (1811-1844). He had poor health throughout his life due to osteomyelitis of the femur so did not go away to school. He was educated at Mr. Bowles' school just off South Quay where James was educated. He was thoughtful and serious, loved entomology and was an excellent artist. With James he wrote the book on the flora and fauna in and around Great Yarmouth. He worked in his father's brewery but his death on 23 March 1844 put to an end any hope of saving the brewery and negotiations for its sale were started the day after his funeral. He did not marry.

Maria Ann Paget (1812-1816).

James Paget (1814-1899).

Francis Paget (1816-1848). He worked with brother Charles in the brewery. He suffered from epilepsy. After the brewery was sold he became a Customs Officer in Liverpool. He was suddenly taken ill on 16 December 1848 and died before

Christmas in the house on South Quay.

Alfred Tolver Paget (1818-1862). He was a school master at Shrewsbury and later became rector of Kirstead, a small village in Norfolk. He did not marry and for a time was looked after by two of his sisters, Patty and Katherine.

Caroline Elizabeth Paget (1819-1820).

Edward Stephen Paget (1820-1821).

Katherine Paget (1825-1885). She did not marry but looked after her parents. When her father died she went to live with her bachelor brother, the Reverend Alfred Paget in Kirstead, Norfolk.

3

EARLY YEARS AND APPRENTICESHIP

James clearly had a happy childhood and along with his brothers and sisters was encouraged to understand the importance of hard work. From his mother he learnt about "orderly arrangement" which he applied so effectively in his later life. He and several of his brothers and sisters also became accomplished artists.

SCHOOLING

James and his brothers attended the local school just off South Quay in Queens Road which was run by a Mr. Bowles who had been an actor. He gave up acting after his wife, who was also an actress, died. He became Minister of the Unitarian Chapel and married again. There were 30 to 35 boys at the school of whom 8 to 10 boarded. The school hours were from 9 a.m. until 12 noon and from 2 to 5 p.m. There were half holidays on Saturdays and sometimes on Mondays when they would be taken for walks in Gorleston, Caister and Burgh Castle.

Site of Mr. Bowles School. Entrance is black doorway to right of No Entry sign. (Dr. Paul Davies)

The school fees were eight guineas a year. James was not impressed by the teaching but his elder brothers did obtain places at Charterhouse School in London. Unfortunately, when James was 13 years of age his father's failing businesses meant that the family could not afford to let him follow his brothers to Charterhouse so he and his three younger brothers continued their education with Mr. Bowles. In his last year at the school, James was head boy but for the rest of his life he felt disadvantaged in not having had a better education. He felt it prevented him in taking part in "learned table-talk."

Woolsey's Mill, near Yarmouth. By James Paget.
(Wellcome Library, London)

At the age of 15 years James considered joining the Royal Navy. He was impressed by the attention the smartly dressed naval officers received, especially from the ladies while walking in Yarmouth. In addition, he appreciated that it was a profession for gentlemen, education was cheap - considering his father's poor finances at this time - and his father had friends in the navy. He therefore studied navigation and extra mathematics and geometry. Just before James's sixteenth birthday Samuel Paget wrote to Captain Sir Eaton Travers asking him to help his son join the navy. His mother was very much against the idea, even though his uniform had been bought. His father decided to sleep on the matter and the next morning the letter was burnt. In later life James admitted that he was very relieved by the decision and felt he would not have made a success in the navy.

APPRENTICESHIP
Following the decision that he would not join the navy it was

decided that he would enter the medical profession although there appears to be no reason for this decision. However, he may have been influenced by the health problems he had seen at home and around the town. He would also have had many contacts with the family doctor who treated several of his brothers and sisters. He was, therefore, apprenticed to Mr. Charles Costerton who was the family doctor and a local surgeon who had trained at St. Bartholomew's Hospital in London. He had been mayor of Yarmouth in 1825. For 100 guineas James was to learn the art and mystery of a surgeon and apothecary over a period of five years. The document for this was signed on 9 March 1830. Normally, Mr. Costerton had several apprentices but in 1830 James was the only one so he had the benefit of having more of his master's time to guide him.

He felt that the course did not need to be as long as five years and that much of the work was tedious. He had to be in the surgery from 9 a.m. until 12 noon and from 2 or 3 p.m. until 5 or 6 p.m. every day. During this time he would be dispensing, seeing a few patients 'of the poorer classes', taking messages, making appointments and keeping accounts. At Christmas time he would have to make out bills. On Mr. Costerton's return from his visits James recorded details of each patient seen and then he had to make up the prescriptions. This might involve preparing liquids and putting them into bottles or rolling pills. For others, leeches would be put in their boxes.

The conditions he saw and treated were ulcerated legs, which required bandaging, coughs, colds and some minor injuries. A fashionable treatment was bleeding and many people thought there was a benefit in having this done once or twice a year, usually in the spring and autumn. Often the patients came after they had spent the day in the market and would be bled until they fainted or nearly did so. They would then return home which, in many cases, was several miles into the country. Years later James remarks that he has no evidence that the procedure did any harm or even any good.

During his time with Dr. Costerton he read a great deal and dissected some amputated limbs. In his second year he had extra anatomy lessons with Mr. Randall, a young surgeon from

Acle, which is a small town ten miles west of Yarmouth. The fourteen lessons were attended by six to eight young apprentices and were given in the Angel Inn in Yarmouth Market Place. The Angel was one of the oldest coaching inns in the town having been rebuilt in 1652. James was very impressed by the standard of Mr. Randall's teaching and his note book in which he wrote down the lessons is in the Royal College of Surgeons of England. His notes are beautifully written and appear to be taken down word for word. It is rare to see a correction or crossing out in his writing. He also had the opportunity of witnessing some of the local surgeons operating whose abilities were very varied. The first major operation he witnessed was on a young man who had been shot in the knee and arm by the large swivel gun on the bow of a boat. The operation involved amputating both limbs without the benefit of anaesthetic and James admitted feeling faint at the experience.

In 1832 there was an outbreak of cholera in the town and James saw various vain attempts at treating it: bleeding, calomel and opium. Saline injections were also tried and one lady was seen to have a temporary improvement while the saline was flowing.

STUDY OF BOTANY

During his apprenticeship he found time to study the local fauna and flora with his brother Charles. Both had been influenced by their mother's love of collecting and orderly arrangement. James was more interested in botany and was encouraged by Mr. Palgrave, a nephew of Dawson Turner who was a banker and a business colleague of Samuel Paget. Another supporter was Sir William Hooker, FRS (1785-1865). He was born in Norwich and was a widely travelled botanist who became Regius Professor of Botany at Glasgow University and subsequently the first director of the Royal Botanic Gardens, Kew. He married Maria, Dawson Turner's eldest daughter, in 1815 and through this connection James was able to correspond with him about specimens he had found. Charles was more interested in entomology, the study of insects.

James collected his specimens on Saturday afternoons and

often before breakfast. His father had an extensive library and it was from the books here that he was able to recognise the plants he had collected and catalogue them. Charles collected the insects while James did this for all the other animals besides the plants. In November 1834 they published their results in a book entitled "A Sketch of the Natural History of Yarmouth and its Neighbourhood, containing Catalogues of the Species of Animals, Birds, Reptiles, Fish, Insects and Plants at present known." It gives the names of 766 insects, 729 flowering plants and 456 non-flowering plants.

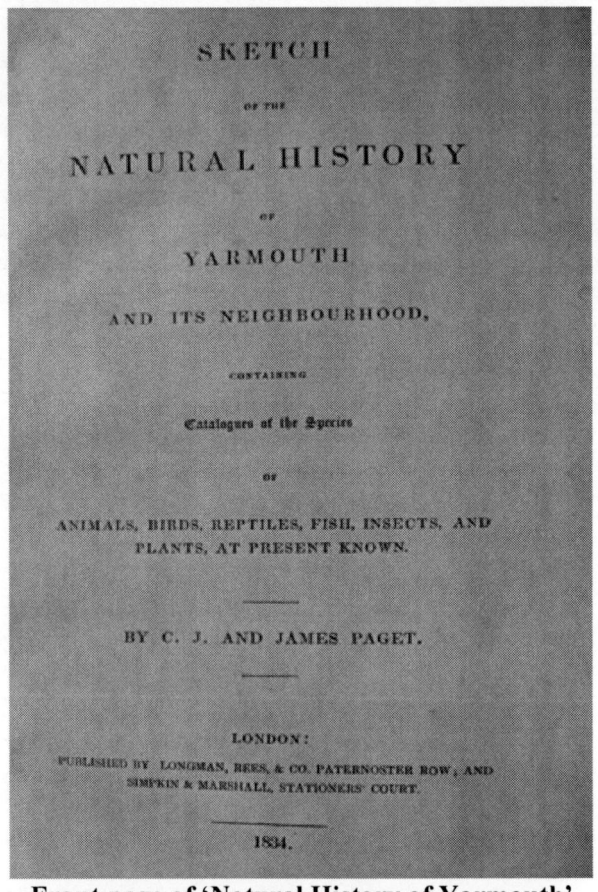

Front page of 'Natural History of Yarmouth'
James wrote the introduction of 32 pages and he is certain

that the work for this book was the greatest influence on his future life. "I think it impossible to estimate too highly the influence of the study of botany on the course of my life. It introduced me into the society of studious and observant men; it gave me an ambition for success, or at the worst some opportunities for display in subjects that were socially harmless; it encouraged the habit of observing, of really looking at things and learning the value of exact descriptions; it educated me in habits of orderly arrangement. I can think of none among the reasons for my success - so far as I can judge of them - which may not be thought of as due in some degree to this part of my apprentice-life. My early associations with scientific men; my readiness to work patiently in museums, and arrange them, and make catalogues; the unfelt power of observing and of recording fact; these and many more helps towards happiness and success may justly be ascribed to the pursuit of botany.

"And, as I look back, I am amused in thinking that of the mere knowledge gained in the study - the knowledge of the appearances and names and botanical arrangements of plants - none had in my after-life any measure of what is called practical utility. The knowledge was useless: the discipline of acquiring it was beyond price."

Apart from the study of the local flora and fauna he taught himself French and had lessons in painting from John Chrome and his son. His brothers Charles and Alfred were very accomplished artists but James learnt enough to illustrate his lectures with good drawings and some of his sketches of pathological specimens were displayed in St. Bartholomew's museum. He preferred drawing and painting to sport but took part in balls, fairs, races, regattas and other social activities.

4

STUDENT AT ST. BARTHOLOMEW'S HOSPITAL

In October 1834 James went to St. Bartholomew's Hospital to study medicine. It was the oldest hospital in London having been founded at a swampy place called Smithfield in 1123 by a monk named Rahere.

St. Bartholomew's Front Quadrangle

    This hospital was chosen for several reasons; it was where Dr. Costerton and his cousin Dr. Moor had trained. In addition, his brother George, who had been elected to a medical fellowship at Caius College Cambridge, had several friends studying there. George's position at Cambridge enabled James to be introduced to some influential friends and George helped out financially by lending him £100 to pay for his entrance fees, lectures and practicals as by this time their father was in severe financial difficulties. From October until Christmas that year he lodged with his brother, George, at 9 Charlotte Street,

Bloomsbury. George had obtained his Batchelor of Medicine degree in Cambridge in 1833 and was doing his clinical studies at St. Bartholomew's Hospital. After Christmas James shared lodgings at 12 Thavies Inn with his friend Dr. Johnstone, a fellow of Caius College Cambridge, and some years his senior. He died a few years later of typhus.

Medical Schools attached to the large London Hospitals arose out of the habit of medical students following surgeons and physicians on their ward rounds. Later, museums of anatomical and surgical specimens were started and surgeons began giving lectures in the operating theatre. They were in competition with the private schools run by such people as William and John Hunter. However, great surgeons such as Percivall Pott (1714-1788), who described a type of ankle fracture, tuberculosis of the spine and cancer of the scrotum in chimney sweeps caused by the soot they were exposed to, made St. Bartholomew's Hospital Medical School successful. Another surgeon, John Abernethy (1764-1831), was an excellent lecturer but not a great surgeon. He was really the founder of the medical school and as a result of his popular teaching the governors built a lecture theatre for him in 1791. However, after he retired in 1827, the medical school started declining. None of the teachers had the ability nor inclination to make it work. Little guidance was given to the students who were left to their own devices. There was a small library next to the operating theatre and the mortuary, which was called the dead house, was in a kind of shed with a stone floor and was damp and dirty. Little instruction was given and pathology was rarely considered.

By contrast the Museum, which had been opened in 1726, was clean and well run. Retired Surgeon Abernethy and Stanley had given their private collections to the hospital. Stanley was the Anatomy Lecturer and in charge of the museum and was very keen to expand the collection. The curator of the museum was Mr. Bayntin who was very good at dissecting and drawing but appears not to have exerted himself.

James felt that the lectures given at the medical school were of varying quality but that the best were given by a Mr. Lawrence at 7 p.m. three days a week on the principles and practice of surgery. Lectures on Anatomy and Physiology were given every day at 2.30 p.m. except Saturday by Mr. Stanley who appeared to have little knowledge of Physiology and only a basic understanding of Anatomy. He had come from a poor background and was ridiculed as a student and teacher yet James was impressed by his honesty and determination to do his best. Another lecturer was Dr. Hue who was the Senior Physician at the hospital. He taught on alternate mornings on the principles and practice of Medicine and on Chemistry and some aspects of Physics. Although he was an impressive speaker his knowledge was out of date and the lectures were poorly attended. He discouraged students attending his ward rounds but James, being the brother of a Cambridge man, was invited. He was rich and carried great power and influence in the hospital and medical school.

Tommy Wormald was the senior demonstrator in anatomy and gave his lectures each morning. He was a Yorkshireman and the most popular of teachers. However, as James worked with Stanley and Lawrence, whom Wormald disliked, he disliked James as well and later was the main opponent in James's advancement in the medical school. Midwifery appeared to be unpopular with James and he attended only two lectures.

Young James felt that he learnt more from reading than he did from the lectures he attended. Most mornings he spent many hours dissecting and almost every evening was devoted to reading, many of the books written in French and German. Apart from having a great desire to learn he did not have the money to socialise. However, his efforts were rewarded when at the end of his first year at medical school he came first in the examinations for Medicine, Surgery, Chemistry and Botany. The prizes he received were Berzelius's Treatise on Chemistry, Baillie's Morbid Anatomy and an edition of Humboldt's Plantae Aequinoctiales.

Another of his achievements in his first year was the discovery of Trichina spiralis on 2 February 1835. Particles of calcium had been noted in human muscle for some time but it was James who looked more closely and discovered the worm in its capsule in the diaphragm of a man of 56 years old. He said

44

"all the men in the dissecting-rooms, teachers included 'saw' the little specks in the muscles: but I believe that I alone 'looked-at' them and 'observed' them: no one trained in natural history could have failed to do so." He examined the specks with his hand lens but this was not powerful enough to see clearly. The hospital did not have a microscope but he obtained an introduction through Dawson Turner of Yarmouth to Mr. Children, the chief of the Natural History Department of the British Museum. Mr. Children took him to see Robert Brown and with his microscope he was able to make sketches of the worm which he used to illustrate the paper he gave to the Hospital's Abernethian Society on 6 February 1835. The same day that he made his discovery he wrote a letter to his brother George telling him about it.

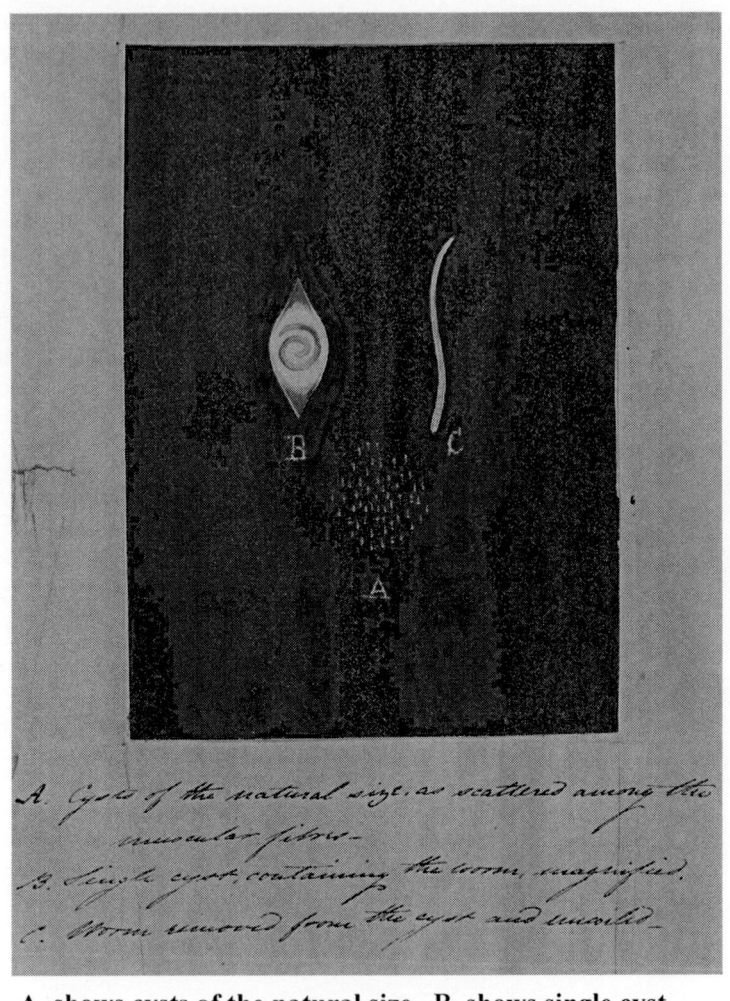

A. shows cysts of the natural size. B. shows single cyst containing worm, magnified. C. worm removed from cyst and uncoiled.
(Royal College of Surgeons)

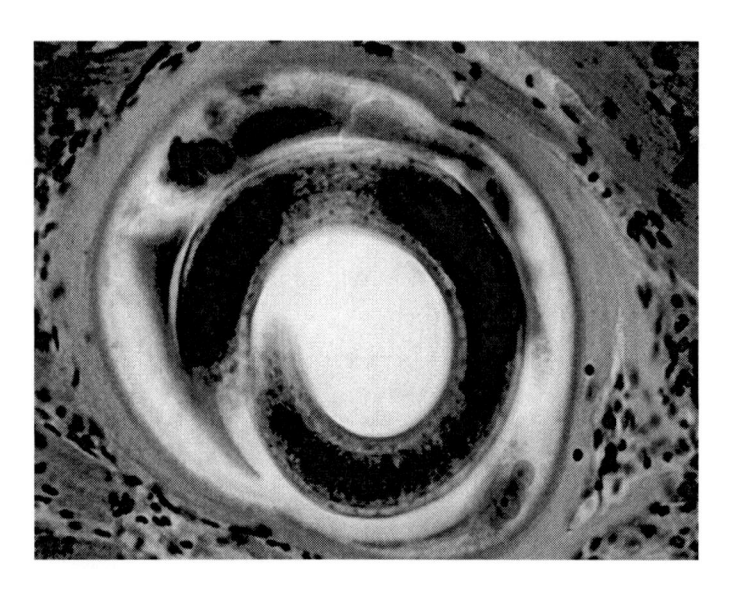

Encysted worm in muscle seen under the microscope

Unbeknown to James, Tommy Wormald took some further specimens to Richard Owen, who gave a series of lectures on Comparative Anatomy at St. Bartholomew's and was assistant curator at the Royal College of Surgeons. He also noted the tiny worms under his microscope - presumably at the Royal College of Surgeons as St. Bartholomew's did not have a microscope - and reported the findings to the Zoological Society. He named the worm Trichina spiralis and took much of the credit for discovering it yet it was a first year medical student who had been the first to see it. In a letter James wrote to Dr. William Hooker (Knighted in 1836) on 16 April he mentions that he had come across the worm in another patient at autopsy and "not being well acquainted with the subject I thought it best that it should be described by some one of more authority than myself, and Mr. Owen, of the Royal College of Surgeons, read a paper on it at the Zoological Society, giving it the name of Trichina spiralis".

Richard Owen (1804-1892) is an interesting and controversial figure and in spite of appearing to take the honour of discovering Trinchina spiralis he became a lifelong friend of

James Paget. Owen was born in Lancaster and, after being apprenticed to a surgeon and apothecary, he went to study Medicine at Edinburgh University in 1824.

Rahere Ward at St. Bartholomew's 1832
(© St. Bartholomew's Hospital Archives)

The following year he went to St. Bartholomew's Hospital to complete his medical studies. After qualifying he did some teaching at the hospital and was advised by surgeon John Abernethy to become assistant to William Clift, Conservator of the museum at the Royal College of Surgeons. He was Hunterian Professor at the College in 1836 and succeeded Clift as Conservator where he was involved in cataloguing some of the Hunterian Collection of specimens. In 1856 he was appointed Superintendent of the Natural History Department of the British Museum. He felt it was important that there should be a special building devoted to Natural History and was responsible for what eventually became known as the Natural History Museum. Throughout his career he was accused of claiming other people's work as his own but he was elected a

Fellow of the Royal Society and was knighted. He worked on many of the specimens brought back by Darwin but they eventually fell out and Owen was despised by many of his former colleagues.

Robert Brown (1773-1858), who had lent James his microscope, was later knighted and is noted for his discovery of the "Brownian movement" of Pollen grains on water. Many years later it was demonstrated that humans become infected with the worm by eating contaminated, poorly cooked meat such as pork.

In the summer months there were no lectures in the medical school so James returned to his home in Yarmouth. This enabled him to see his family and friends and saved him spending money on his lodgings. In his memoirs Paget could not remember how he spent his time that summer but no doubt he spent much of it reading, walking in the countryside and on the beaches and talking with Dr. Costerton, Dawson Turner and other learned men. His notebooks in the Royal College of Surgeons show that part of the time was spent helping Dr. William Travers Cox with postmortems and he records in great detail the history of the events leading up to death and the findings at postmortem. On 16 August, 1835 there was a postmortem on an 8 year old child who had died the preceding evening after swallowing some carbonate of potash thinking it was beer. On 9 September he helped Dr. Cox with a postmortem on a four month old boy.

Dr. Cox was born in Ireland and obtained a Bachelor of Arts degree at Trinity College, Dublin in 1828 and an MA in 1832. He then studied medicine at Pembroke College, Oxford. He practiced medicine in Great Yarmouth from the early 1830s and was appointed physician to the Yarmouth General Hospital in 1838. However, he resigned two years later as he found that the surgeons were treating patients with medical conditions and sometimes left their students to treat their patients.

In his second year James attended few lectures and spent his time reading, dissecting and attending patients on the wards and in clinics. He did not have the 10 guineas to become a dresser and the post of house surgeon was even more expensive so he spent most of his time on the medical wards preparing for the examinations. He attended the ward rounds of the Physician, Dr. Peter Mere Latham, who taught him and about a dozen other students how to examine patients, how to learn and how to make careful notes.

Early in 1836 he moved from the Thavies Inn to share lodgings at 82 Hatton Garden with his friends Firth and Master who came from Norwich.

Again he triumphed in the medical examinations coming first in Anatomy and Physiology, Clinical Medicine and Medical Jurisprudence. This last subject he had learnt in four to five days by reading Beck's large Medical Jurisprudence. His father came to the prize giving on 11 May and was immensely proud of his son's achievements and the praise that he received from his tutors.

On the 13 May 1836 he passed the College of Surgeons' Membership Examination, which he thought was very simple, just 19 months after entering St. Bartholomew's. One of the examiners was the President of the Royal College of Surgeons, Sir Astley Cooper (1768-1841), who spent his teenage years in Great Yarmouth. Astley Cooper said that he knew Samuel Paget and claimed that they had fought when they were boys although James denied that. He said that the President invited him to breakfast but whether he accepted is not known.

Sir Astley Cooper. Statue by Baily in St. Paul's Cathedral
(Dr. Paul Davies)

It is interesting comparing Paget and Astley Cooper. Both came from the same town but Astley Cooper was 46 years older, had a securer financial backing and his uncle was a surgeon at Guy's Hospital where he became a surgeon. He was much more flamboyant than the more serious Paget and he described the anatomy of hernias, ligaments in the breast and performed operations on aneurysms - dilatations of arteries which can rupture - in the neck, leg and abdomen without any form of anaesthetic. Both had enquiring minds, worked extremely hard, became President of the Royal College of Surgeons, Fellow of the Royal Society and were the leading surgeons of their day.

5

NEWLY QUALIFIED DOCTOR

The accepted route to becoming a surgeon at a London Hospital was through serving up to five years as a surgical dresser. James could not afford the fee for this position so this route was not open to him and he always felt that this lack of surgical experience as a student and after qualifying was a disadvantage and hindered his surgical expertise.

When James qualified as a doctor science played only a small part in medicine. There was little attempt at making a diagnosis and doctors treated symptoms. They gave medicines made from plants and treated syphilis and other diseases with mercury which probably did more harm than good. Bleeding was popular but had no proven benefit. Surgery was confined to amputations, treating fractures, draining abscesses and cysts and removing tumours. There were no anaesthetics, although some patients were given alcohol or preparations of opium which helped to dull the pain. Occasionally patients were bled to the point of fainting before an operation so that they were less likely to be aware of the operation. Patients had to be very stoical and were often tied down to a couch or held down by some strong men. The cause of infection was not known and little attempt was made to clean instruments. If the patient survived the operation, and did not die of blood loss, they frequently succumbed later from infection. Operations required the bravery of both the surgeon and the patient.

Following his successes in his examinations, James returned to Great Yarmouth for four months. His options were to go into partnership with one of the local surgeons or to return to London in the hope that a job would "turn up." He returned to London in October 1836 and his father agreed to give him £10 monthly for the following six months if he was unable to earn a living. At the same time he became engaged to Lydia North whom he had known for nearly two years but they would have to wait another eight years before they were able to marry. He had first met her in Yarmouth where two of her brothers were curates and friends of the Paget family. Their father, Reverend Henry North, who was domestic chaplain to the Duke of York, lived at 1 Cornwall Terrace, Regent's Park and James frequently went there on a Sunday. James's father disapproved of the engagement and told him so in a letter dated 23 November 1836 as he had no prospect of an adequate income.

James took lodgings at 2 Millman Street, Bedford Row in London and took on a student who boarded with him for £10 monthly. Unfortunately, the student was unable to work and after four months James asked him to leave and took himself off to Paris for three months - from January to March - having asked his father for £10 a month. He met up with some men from St. Bartholomew's and listened to various talks and lectures by famous men but was not very impressed by his time in Paris. He found the French medical students "the most ruffianly, ill-looking set of fellows I ever saw....wooden shoes, ragged coats and unwashed and unshaved faces are the ornaments of a large majority." He thought that surgical practice in France was inferior to that in England yet France was superior in the science of Medicine.

Returning to London in April 1837 he took on some students to help them prepare for their examinations. In the following three to four years there were only 8-10 students in total and he became rather despondent with this form of teaching. He preferred writing and was subeditor of the Medical Gazette for nearly five years. He would write leading articles every two to three weeks on medical education, scientific progress, recent discoveries etc. His main work was reporting lectures, reviews and translations from French, German, Dutch and Italian. He also wrote on debates at the Medico-Chirurgical Society and he did this, not by taking notes, but by listening carefully and writing the reports at home afterwards.

He wrote reports for the Quarterly Review and many of these required translation from foreign languages. A large work was the Annual Reports on the Progress of Anatomy and Physiology. This involved him working with Dr. (Later Sir) John Forbes and young Paget felt that a good report from him to his oldest friend, Sir James Clark, led to his later appointment of Surgeon Extraordinary to Queen Victoria at such a young age. James Clark had been physician to the Duchess of Kent whose daughter became Queen Victoria in July 1937. Soon afterwards he was appointed Queen Victoria's physician-in-ordinary and received a baronetcy.

He also wrote for the Penny Cyclopaedia and the Biographical Dictionary. In the former he wrote most of the articles on human anatomy, physiology and surgery and in the latter he wrote the biographies of many famous people. This work taught him a great deal for, as he said in his Memoirs, "I had, before this, known very little of the history of medicine: I ended with knowing not much more, but with a clear impression of the immense difficulty of writing an accurate and nearly complete history of any time or science; and with a thorough disregard for all histories written lightly or prettily. Besides, I learnt more than ever the value or necessity of always referring, if possible, to the very book, volume, and page quoted from, or from which any statement is made, and the similar necessity of verifying every reference made from another. Nothing could better teach the difficulty, the necessity, and rarity of accuracy in writing than did this work in biography."

During this time he worked very long hours, up to one or two o'clock in the morning. He was short of money and usually went without dinner on Fridays. He found that dates and raisins could overcome the feeling of hunger. These long hours and poor diet led to him developing pneumonia in August 1837. This was the first of several attacks of pneumonia he had over many years.

From 1837 to 1843 he was Curator of St. Bartholomew's Museum. At St. Bartholomew's, the position of Curator was a lowly one although at Guy's Dr. Hodgkin held that position as did Owen at the College of Surgeons. The situation at St. Bartholomew's was very different and he spent much time trying to incorporate into the title Assistant Demonstrator of Anatomy or Demonstrator of Morbid Anatomy. This was not to be and eventually he accepted the post of Curator in the hope that it might lead to further posts at the hospital.

Much of the work was mundane but at least it gave him a wage of £100 in the first year although the following year it was reduced to £40 yearly, probably because he refused to give an undertaking not to do any other work and to give an assurance that he would hold the post for a number of years. Work was from 9 in the morning to 4 in the afternoon five days a week, though when his pay was reduced it was agreed that he would not work in the Museum in the mornings which would give him the opportunity of earning money from other sources.

Work in the Museum involved organising the specimens, getting them ready for lectures, sketching specimens and arranging the lectures. However, it allowed him to see the changes brought on by disease, it prepared him for the post of Demonstrator in Morbid Anatomy and the clerical jobs involved in being the Warden of the hospital's new college. It enabled him to write a new catalogue of the Museum which led to him being appointed to write the Pathological Catalogue of the College of Surgeons Museum. This led to him being appointed to the Professorship of the College. Although these were the advantages, the downside was that he was not able to do any surgery until he became surgeon of the Finsbury Dispensary in 1841.

He moved to 3 Serle Street, Lincoln's Inn in January 1838 where he rented rooms on the first floor above Ravenscroft's, a shop supplying barristers with their wigs and gowns. He saw some patients here but his income from this averaged only £13 to £14 annually. This was certainly the low point of his life and carried on for nearly seven years. He spent his time reading, writing and attending to the Museum work. He rarely participated in social activities or took holidays. It made him susceptible to disease and in early 1839 he developed typhus and was ill for three months. A year before, on 27 March, his best friend Johnstone died of the same condition so he felt himself very fortunate to have survived.

In the summer of 1839 he was appointed to the Demonstratorship of Morbid Anatomy which involved doing the medical postmortem examinations. In November many students requested that he give lectures and eventually this was allowed on a weekly basis. Initially they were given in the post mortem room, where the students had to stand, but the following year he was allowed to use the anatomy lecture theatre. He had not lectured before and there was no time to prepare what he was to say so he decided to lecture on the specimens that had been obtained from recent postmortem examinations. He received no payment for these lectures but was encouraged by their popularity among the students.

He was elected Surgeon to the Finsbury Dispensary on 14 April 1841 following an election. He was required to attend the Dispensary at 9.30 a.m. on Mondays, Tuesdays and Fridays and to see and treat outpatients. Two years later on 31 May 1843 he resigned the post on being appointed Lecturer at St. Bartholomew's. In recognition of his work he was appointed an Honorary Life Governor of the Dispensary and later Consulting Surgeon.

In 1841 Wormald resigned from the post of Demonstrator in Anatomy and James was appointed in his place to give demonstrations with McWhinnie at a salary of £100 a year. Unfortunately, there was a dispute as to the fairness of Hospital apprentices having sole right to the post of assistant surgeon. They had paid 500 guineas for the four to five year post of apprentice and 1000 guineas if the post was resident. The position gave them great experience and the post of Demonstrator in Anatomy was regarded as the final step before becoming assistant surgeon. It was felt that James's appointment to this position would go against a long tradition and the appointment was blocked by getting Wormald to withdraw his resignation.

The following year the Council of the Royal College of Surgeons asked Edward Stanley of St. Bartholomew's to suggest someone who could catalogue the specimens in their Hunterian Museum. He suggested James Paget who was doing such an admirable job cataloguing the specimens at St. Bartholomew's. The work was tedious and involved rearranging the collection and incorporating specimens from other collections. He had to study Hunter's writings and illustrations. He described every specimen as he saw it and emphasised the importance of being accurate and not making assumptions. The initial Conservator of the Hunterian Collection was William Clift who, as a young man, had been personal assistant to John Hunter. Richard Owen, who had tried to claim he had discovered Trichina spiralis, resigned the lectureship in comparative anatomy at St. Bartholomew's in 1835 and became Clift's assistant. In 1842 Clift retired and Owen became the Museum's Conservator. Unfortunately, Owen was unhappy about having to work with Paget but the situation was resolved by the decision that Owen would be responsible for the physiology section of the new catalogue while Paget would deal with the pathology. They were able to work well together and in 1856 Owen moved to the British Museum.

Paget continued to write for journals and to lecture to students but his medical and surgical practice was practically nil. He found this particularly hard to bear and on top of this he was trying to deal with his father's increasing debts. However, in 1842 St. Bartholomew's obtained its first microscope and Paget spent many hours studying different tissues and writing up his findings.

Paget lecturing to students
(© St. Bartholomew's Hospital Archives)

In 1843 it was decided to separate the teaching of Anatomy and Physiology, as had been done in other medical schools, and this paved the way for James to be appointed to the newly created post of Lecturer in Physiology on 30 May. His knowledge of the subject had accumulated over the eight years he had worked for the Quarterly Review reporting and reviewing recent advances in physiology. There was more competition for the post of Anatomy Lecturer. It seemed likely that Wormald would be appointed but the post went to Skey who had been the chief teacher at the private school in Aldersgate Street as well as being Assistant Surgeon at St. Bartholomew's. James would lecture five days a week on General Anatomy and Physiology, and on Saturdays he would cover Morbid Anatomy. This continued for six months. His lectures supplied most of the materials for the first edition of Kirkes' Handbook of Physiology published in 1848. Kirkes was one of Paget's brightest students. He was born in Lancashire in 1822 and trained at St. Bartholomew's, eventually becoming a full physician there. He wrote papers on embolism and heart disease. In 1848 he developed pneumononia and pericarditis and died within five days.

James Paget had a reputation as a very great speaker and fine orator. He felt that he was born with this ability but he had to work at it.

For very important lectures or speeches he would spend many hours learning the speech word for word and would spend time rehearsing parts of the speech. For the majority of lectures to students he would not prepare in this way and would usually speak spontaneously. For other talks he would memorize the important parts and fill in the rest as he went along. He said that good preparation was essential for imparting accurate information with clear expression and to do so was just as important as it was for writing.

1843 marked the decline of the medical school to its lowest level and only 36 students entered for the Anatomy lectures. For some time there had been no supervision nor guidance of the students and no-one to oversee their welfare. It was, therefore, decided to introduce the 'Collegiate System' based on the system at Oxford and Cambridge. The idea had come from one of Lydia North's brothers, the Reverend Mr. North who was Chaplain to St. George's Hospital. There was some support for the idea from some of the doctors at St. Bartholomew's and, more particularly, by the hospital treasurer, Mr. James Bentley. Paget was appointed the first college warden on 8 August 1843.

Six houses in Duke Street were renovated and in another a kitchen and dining hall were built. There was accommodation for 23 students and young Paget drew up the rules ready for the College to open in October 1843. He moved into rooms in the College on 28 September having vacated Serle Street. It had been agreed that he would have the rooms rent free and would be paid £75 to £100 for the post of warden. The Collegiate system was very successful, not only in providing accommodation and in supporting its students, but it helped James in his career. He advised nearly all students in their studies and was essentially the treasurer of the College. He became increasingly involved in the running of the medical school and was in the Hospital daily. The College also had the support of the governors which, in the long term, would help the future of the hospital.

His happiness at these positive events was tempered by his mother's illness. Several years earlier she had had a stroke and had become increasingly incapacitated. In the past she had been the dominant person in the house on South Quay; overseeing the education and welfare of her children, the running of the house and giving comfort to her husband in his increasing financial difficulties. In recent years she had become increasingly dependent on others yet made light of her infirmities. James returned to Yarmouth for a month in the latter part of the summer to see his mother and his brother Charles who was also unwell. His mother died on 22 November 1843 and how proud she would have been to know that only days later her son James would be one of 300 foundation Fellows elected to the College of Surgeons from all over the country. He was also the youngest.

These changes caused a complete change in his life style. No longer did he eat alone. Each day he dined in Hall at an upper table reserved for people holding office in the School or Hospital. He also felt free in May 1844 to marry Lydia who had waited for him for eight years. The wedding took place in St. Mary's Church, Bryanston Square, London but was a small and rather sombre affair as his brother, Charles, had died in March after a long illness. The honeymoon consisted of a day's visit to Oxford as they could afford nothing more. He thought it did not match the beauty of Cambridge but he was impressed by some very old paintings in Christ Church.

His brother Charles had been in poor health for many months and died on 23 March 1844. He had helped his father to run the brewery but with his death any chance of saving it was gone and negotiations to sell it started the day after his funeral. It was hoped that the brewery's proximity to the railway (The line from Norwich to Yarmouth opened that year) would increase its value but it was sold in February 1845. It was pulled down soon after the sale and the bricks were used to build a Roman Catholic Church in Yarmouth. With the sale of the brewery, brother Frank had no job and eventually was employed as a custom's officer in Liverpool. His sisters, Patty and Kate, took it in turns to go to Liverpool to keep house for him.

After their wedding James and Lydia lived in the College's two rooms he had before his marriage and a few weeks later they moved into a house bought for the warden. During the evenings Lydia would play and sing while he would write. Later, she would transcribe his notes for lectures and papers written for journals so that they were ready for the printers. They had no spare money and life was spartan. Rarely did they go out to other people's houses for dinner and, if they did, it was not uncommon for them to walk home to save the cost of a cab. However, every Sunday evening they would invite friends and students for a meal and music. Often he and Lydia would walk around the hospital square in the evening and reports by contemporaries say how bright and cheerful he was although in letters to his brothers he seems to dwell on the negative parts of his life.

Gradually he was able to give up writing for the various magazines and journals and concentrate on the running of the College and School, the preparation of his lectures (140 in six months) and the cataloguing of the specimens in the Hospital Museum and the College of Surgeons.

In September 1846 he published 'Records of Harvey in

extracts from the Journals of the Royal Hospital of St. Bartholomew'. It was a 37 page collection of all the entries connected with Harvey in the Hospital Journals with historical notes by James Paget. In October he published the 'Descriptive Catalogue of the Anatomical Museum of St. Bartholomew's Hospital'. It was 487 pages long and described 2,298 specimens of disease or injury along with notes and references.

On October 1 he gave the introductory address to the students 'On the Motives to Industry in the Study of Medicine'. In it he said "We ought all to be united, not only, as we must be, by one law of interest and of responsibility, but by all we have, or should have, in common; by the one pursuit of science, by one zeal for the honour of the school, one desire to maintain unsullied the reputation which we all derive from the great and honourable men who have worked here before us, - by one feeling, that a sordid or unhandsome act of one would be a blot on the fair fame of the whole body."

In spite of his many commitment he still found time to help launch and run a charity for the poor and homeless at the House of Charity founded in 1846. The prime founders were Dr. Henry Monro, who was born in 1817, and Roundell Palmer (1812-1895). Both men graduated from Oxford. Monro spent his life looking after people with mental health problems and worked for the charity helping destitute people for forty years whereas Palmer became a Tory MP in 1847 and later joined the Liberal party. He was elected a fellow of the Royal Society in 1860, held several prominent positions in government and Gladstone appointed him Lord Chancellor in 1872 when he became the first Baron Selborne. Gladstone was also one of the original founders of the charity and in the early days, when there was no resident warden, Paget and Gladstone took their turns to sleep at the house. For Paget it was the start of a fifty year friendship with Gladstone. Even into old age Paget would often go to a service at the charity's chapel. The charity still exists and is called the House of St. Barnabas-in-Soho. Its aim is to provide sustained employment for those affected by homelessness.

6

PROMOTIONS

In January 1847 he was appointed the Professor of Anatomy and Surgery at the College of Surgeons. This was a great honour as the position normally went to a member of Council. It required giving six lectures over two weeks and they were called the Arris and Gale Lectures. He decided to lecture on General Pathology and so successful was the course that he was re-elected for the succeeding five years. The titles for the six years were:

1847   Nutrition
1848   The Life of the Blood
1849   The processes of Repair and Reproduction after Injuries
1850   Inflammation
1851   Tumours
1852   Malignant Tumours

The lectures were designed "to give lectures which might illustrate the general pathology of the principal surgical diseases, in conformity with the larger and more exact doctrines of physiology."

The lectures were extremely well attended, were very successful and helped to spread his reputation. Much of what he discussed he had discovered using his microscope. It was only twelve years previously that St. Bartholomew's did not possess one and he had gone to the British Museum to find one. The lectures showed the breadth and depth of his knowledge, the logic of his thought and resulted in many regarding him as the founder of British Pathology. The lectures were published in the Medical Times and Gazette and were the basis for his 'Lectures in Surgical Pathology" which were published in 1853 in two volumes.

Paget was primarily a pathologist but his knowledge of

Physiology was equally broad. He read extensively in preparing for his five lectures a week and he tested out many of his ideas by experiments he carried out e.g. observing the blood supply in the "wings" of bats, the respiration of tadpoles and finding out why a bird's egg does not freeze many degrees below thirty-two degrees Fahrenheit. It was not only the knowledge he had but the way in which he analysed a problem and presented his views which was so impressive. In recognition of his contributions to Physiology he was one of the few people who were made honorary members of the Physiological Society when it was founded.

One of his pupils, Sir William Turner (1832-1916), was Professor of Anatomy and Principal of Edinburgh University, President of the General Medical Council and of the British Medical Association and was a Fellow of the Royal Society. He summarises many of Paget's attributes in the Edinburgh Medical Journal of November 1901. "Paget had the ability and insight to recognise the value of the microscope in pathology, and his knowledge of modern languages enabled him to keep pace with the investigations of continental writers on normal and morbid histology. When his lectures on Surgical Pathology were published in 1853, they at once took the place of a standard treatise, and they placed the author in the first rank of pathologists both at home and abroad.........Prior to Paget's appointment as a lecturer, the medical school at St. Bartholomew's had been steadily declining, but under the influence of his character and teaching the entry of new students doubled in number, and the school regained its place as one of the first in London. As an expositor of a difficult branch of medical science Paget was facile princeps. His untiring application made him conversant with the progress of his subject in all its details; his quick apprehension of the value of recorded observations, tested daily by his own researches, enabled him to impress on his pupils the facts of primary, and to discriminate those of only secondary, importance; his orderly mind marshalled the facts in logical manner; his keen, eager face, the bright, penetrating eyes, his facility in speaking, his choice of language, and the charm of his delivery, presented the subject so as at once to attract and fix the attention of the large class of students. But in addition his pupils felt that he was earnest in his work, that he was interested in them as individuals, an interest which showed itself both in the words of encouragement which they received during their pupilage, and in the support which he gave them at critical stages of their career in after life. Many will recollect and treasure the kindly look, the warm greeting, the affectionate shake of the hand which they received on meeting him, even years after they had left the school."

In February 1847 there was an election for an Assistant Surgeon at St. Bartholomew's. James Paget's two contenders were Mr. William Pennington and Mr. McWhinnie. Both had been apprentices, dressers and house surgeons and Mr. McWhinnie was a lecturer in comparative anatomy. Therefore, they had a much greater understanding of and experience in surgery and McWhinnie was older and far more senior in the hospital to Paget. Nevertheless, the President, the Treasurer and most of the influential governors supported the young Paget. Consequently, he was appointed with a convincing majority yet he had not done one operation in private practice in the last nine years.

With this appointment he saw 180 to 220 patients daily for a salary of £100 annually. He decided to give up the £50 salary as Warden as it was paid for by contributions of the medical officers and lecturers. He performed his first operation in public in April and, considering his lack of surgical experience, this must have been a daunting occasion for him.

1847 also marked the introduction of anaesthesia. James Young Simpson (1811-1870) was an obstetrician and professor of Medicine and Midwifery at Edinburgh University. He presented his paper on ether at a meeting of the Royal Medical Society of Edinburgh and very soon afterwards ether was being used at St. Bartholomew's for the extraction of teeth. His next paper in November showed the advantages of chloroform over ether for operations, and within three years over seven thousand anaesthetics had been given at St. Bartholomew's.

This was very good timing for Paget as it meant that within a year of him being appointed Assistant Surgeon he no longer had to operate on patients without the benefit of anaesthesia. In letters to his brother George in 1849 he says that on 23 January he did a "formidable operation on Saturday....Thank God I got well through it, and the patient is making good progress; but it was one the hardest cases of tumour I have seen meddled with." On 27 March he writes "I performed my first lithotomy on Saturday - slowly and not, perhaps, too dexterously - but not confusedly - and, as I hope, very safely, for the boy is doing well." It is likely that both operations were done under chloroform. Lithotomy means 'cutting for stone' and had been practiced for over 2,000 years to remove stones from the bladder. Up until that time, about half the patients died from blood loss and sepsis and, of those who survived, many were left incontinent of urine.

Back in Yarmouth the contents of his father's house were being sold. First to go were the more valuable paintings which were sold in London in August 1847 and over the following months other items were sold. Eventually, in October 1848 all the remaining contents of the house were sold in a three-day auction. Apart from the sadness of loosing all their possessions with so many memories the money which was received for them was pitiful. The family decided to have one last Christmas in the old house although it was empty. Each would bring some food and drink. Unfortunately, on 16 December Frank was suddenly taken ill and died within a few days at the age of 32 years, so Christmas was an even more sombre affair than expected.

Samuel Paget and his daughters finally left the house on 14 February 1849 and it appears to have been unoccupied until 1859 when it became the Government Schools of Art and Navigation. Subsequently it became the School of Science and Art, managed by the Corporation of Yarmouth, until it was bombed in 1941. The house was subsequently razed to the ground but a plaque commemorating the fact that Sir James Paget had been born there which had been fixed to the wall of the house was saved and was incorporated into the block of flats which were built on the site in the 1950s.

In spite of the loss of his house, its possessions and his dignity, Samuel Paget had great satisfaction in being given a pension by the Shipping Clubs of Yarmouth. Not only was the money useful but the award recognised the service he had given to them over nearly 50 years as Treasurer and President. Nevertheless, he still had enormous debts and in April 1849 George, James and Alfred met and agreed to pay off their father's debts and to give a small income to their father and his daughters. Each signed a legal document to bind them to this agreement and it was not until 1862 that all the debts were repaid. For each of them it caused a great deal of financial hardship especially in the early years.

On a happier note, James completed the Pathological Catalogue of the College of Surgeons Museum in May 1849 after seven years hard work. It consisted of 1,218 pages with descriptions of 3,520 specimens. It replaced the 1830 catalogue produced by Mr. Clift and incorporated the many specimens which had been donated or been bought from private collections such as those of Sir Astley Cooper and Liston, so more than doubling the number of specimens in the Museum. Mr. Clift identified John Hunter's original specimens, Paget described all the specimens in meticulous detail and Mr. Edward Stanley - who had been one of Paget's lecturers at St. Bartholomew's, had supported him over the years and recommended him for the post of cataloguing the specimens - reviewed what had been written and approved it.

Hunterian Museum in about 1860. Water colour by TH Shepherd
(Royal College of Surgeons)

The Medical School continued to improve each year following the formation of the College and the number of students had more than doubled. In 1843 there were 44 and by 1851 they had risen to 106.

Paget was responsible for a woman being allowed to study medicine at the hospital. She was Elizabeth Blackwell who, after being born in Bristol in 1821, emigrated with her family to New York State at the age of eleven. She had great difficulty in being accepted by a medical school, but eventually qualified in 1849 as a doctor of medicine at Geneva College, Geneva which is a small town in the Ontario and Seneca counties in the state of New York. She decided to further her studies in Europe but the only post she could obtain was that of student midwife at the La Maternite in Paris. One day while syringing pus from the eyes of a new born baby the infected liquid splashed into her left eye. This led to a severe infection resulting in the loss of sight in that eye which was eventually removed and replaced by a glass eye.

While recovering from this operation a cousin of Dr. Blackwell approached James Paget and he managed to obtain the permission of the St. Bartholomew's House Committee to let her study at the medical school from October 1850. He wrote her a letter of welcome and she was invited to breakfast at the Paget's house along with about twelve students. Before she attended her first pathology lecture Paget asked the all male class to accept her and Dr. Blackwell subsequently said "When I entered and bowed I received a round of applause. My seat is always reserved for me and I have no trouble. There are, I think, about sixty students, the most gentlemanly class I have seen."

Paget wrote notes on all his students at this time and said of Dr. Blackwell: "The celebrated Dr. Blackwell - a sensible, quiet, discreet lady - she gained a fair knowledge (not more) of medicine, practised in New York, then tried to promote female doctordom in England."

1851 was marked by the Great Exhibition and the birth of James and Lydia's second soon, Francis. James was elected to the Fellowship of the Royal Society which was recognition for his outstanding work in pathology and physiology. There were 38 candidates for the fellowship of which 15 were selected and at the first election he was the only candidate for whom the whole council voted. Between 1854 and 1889 he served on the Society's Council five times which was a most unusual honour.

In July he gave a lecture at the Royal College of Surgeons on 'The Recent Progress of Anatomy and its influence on Surgery'. He showed how the use of the microscope could demonstrate the histology of tissues and how important was a knowledge of pathology and biochemistry. "It would be impossible to name a department of medicine or surgery, to which the recent studies of anatomy have not contributed, at least, useful facts. The pathology of inflammation, the repair of injuries, the production and development of morbid growths, the whole of that vast field upon which medicine and surgery meet and mutually illustrate one another - all these have been illustrated by direct observations with the modern methods of research....Modern anatomy has adopted not only new methods, but even new objects of research; it has not only extended itself largely in its recognised territory, but, much more, has passed into wholly new fields of enquiry - with the microscope, with chemistry, and with enlarged comparisons of lower forms and types of structure."

He goes on "It would not be difficult to point out a large number of cases in which we may well hope for progress by these means. In regard to such a disease as cancer, for example, we want to know the proportion of cases in which cancer returns after operation, the average time that a patient lives upon whom no operation is performed, the average age, and all other circumstances connected with the disease; and I would venture to say, that whole volumes of statistics as yet recorded upon the matter, nay, that almost every statistical table yet printed is simply and wholly valueless for these purposes, and valueless, chiefly because of the non-use of those means by which alone we can detect what is and what is not a cancer. The microscope must be used, with all other methods of research, before we can approach the knowledge of one of those truths for want of which we are constantly practising in doubt, still casting upon the patient the responsibility we ought to take upon ourselves, still leaving things unsettled which have been unsettled for centuries past."

Finally, he stresses the importance of knowledge and not just dexterity in performing surgery. "We must not forget that the emergencies of surgery are more those of the mind than of the hand. The dextrous hand is indeed a noble gift; he who wears it, wears the best mark of human form, an admirable symbol and instrument of humanity ... But much better than the dextrous hand is the instructed mind, clear, strong, resolute, and pliant, experienced in struggles against difficulty - such a mind as can be educated only in the intricacies of some hard science."

Although his life had been transformed by his promotions

and marriage he did not enjoy dealing with students who were lazy, noisy or overspent their allowances. He was now earning five to six hundred pounds annually but he felt that this would not be enough to educate his children so, after seven years as Warden, he resigned in October 1851 and entered surgical practice. The family moved to 24 Henrietta Street, Cavendish Square.

7

PRIVATE PRACTICE

In October 1851 he took on private practice more or less full time. Before then he had seen the occasional private patient and operated on only a few. In the first seven years after qualifying his largest annual salary was only £23. 13s and in the succeeding years it never exceeded £100. The reasons for taking on private practice were probably financial and professional. From a financial point of view he was struggling to provide for his enlarging family as well as having to pay off his Father's debts with two of his brothers. His finances were a great worry to him and frequently he referred to them in letters to his brother George as did his wife, Lydia. Because of this he would regularly walk long distances to give lectures rather than go by cab or public transport. The couple rarely attended social functions and, if they did, frequently they would walk home.

From a professional point of view he had been Professor at the Royal College of Surgeons for nearly six years and as a result of his lectures he was about to publish a highly successful book on Pathology. He was still giving lectures on Physiology and these required much work in their preparation and he found he had less time to carry out his physiological experiments. His work as Warden at the College had seen the reputation of the Medical School drastically improve but the position of warden carried with it many responsibilities which he was finding increasingly difficult to maintain. In addition, he did not like having to remonstrate with idle and often noisy students. As for his hospital work he found it increasingly difficult to maintain the high standards he had set himself with all his other commitments. Often he covered for others and did more than his fair share of practical work in the outpatients' room and on the wards.

However, probably the most important reason was that he wanted to be a surgeon. Lack of money and connections had made it impossible for him to take up this option after qualifying so he had devoted all his energies into Pathology and Physiology and had spent hours every week dissecting and carrying out postmortems. He knew his ability and determination to tackle problems, he had a vast knowledge of human anatomy, he understood diseases and their consequences and he was one of the few medical people in the country who had such a command of so many European languages that he was up to date with the latest advances on the continent. No one in London was so uniquely medically qualified and he wanted to use his knowledge, his abilities and his resolve to overcome problems to progress the science of surgery.

Leaving the Warden's house they moved to 24 Henrietta Street, Cavendish Square in 1852 and in his first year he earned £400. His income increased yearly to more than £10,000 but fell to £7,000 when he gave up operating. For many years he was regarded as the best surgeon to see in London and consequently had the most lucrative practice. He regarded his success as being due to his reputation, honesty, hard work and being businesslike. He was naturally civil, polite and punctual. Patients were referred to him by his senior colleagues at St. Bartholomew's, by his previous students and, as his reputation grew, patients also asked to be referred to him. An example of this was that, following his treatment of the Princess of Wales, his practice more than doubled.

Although he had given up many of his previous responsibilities he continued to work very hard. He would visit the hospital at least six days a week and never refused to attend to urgent cases irrespective of the time of day or night. As a result, he had a very strict timetable. He would perform private operations and visit the more important cases between 8 and 10 in the morning after which he would see 15 to 20 patients at his home over three hours. Following this he would attend the hospital for between one hour and up to two and a half hours after which he would visit private patients around London. It would be 7 o'clock or later before he returned home for dinner, after which he would write letters, attend to his patients' notes or do some reading. Rarely did he retire to bed before midnight. Occasionally he was required to give opinions on patients in other parts of the country. This could interrupt his schedule but was usually well paid and by this time the rapidly expanding railway system was a big help.

In early 1853 he had one of several attacks of pneumonia which he suffered during his life. Lydia was concerned for his health and the pressures that he put himself under e.g. walking through the rain to give lectures rather than taking the omnibus. Although he recovered from the chest infection, later in the year he wrote to his brother, George, on 17 September "I am, this year, utterly overladen; my pocket, as you too well know, is more than emptied; my health is blown upon; and I seem at last to need even rest of mind. I cannot bear more responsibility. If it were not for your confidence, I sometimes think that my hope might fail."

However, by the following year his situation was improving and he was considering buying a brougham for his wife. In January 1854 he was elected a member of the Philosophical Society of Philadelphia and in June he started a course of lectures at the Royal Institution entitled "The importance of the study of Physiology as a branch of education for all classes."

In August he was appointed as an examiner of candidates for 'assistant-surgeoncies' in the East India Company at an initial fee of £100 annually. There were three other examiners - Dr. Parkes to examine in medicine, Mr. Busk in anatomy and Sir Joseph Hooker to examine in general science. They met for two weeks each year. Sir Joseph Hooker (1817-1911) was the younger son of Sir William who had helped James when he was studying botany in his teens. Sir Joseph was assistant director of the Royal Botanic Gardens at Kew from 1855 until 1865 when he succeeded his father as director, a post he held until 1885.

The four examiners were appalled at the lack of knowledge of the candidates in spite of the fact that a condition of entry to the examination was that they had to be members of one of the three surgical colleges. Apart from written papers, Paget oversaw the candidates performing a major and a minor operation on cadavers. Their lack of knowledge and ability was shocking and many were failed. This caused consternation at the Colleges as it challenged the standards they had set in their examinations and it resulted in the East India Company being unable to fill their surgical vacancies. Much of the blame for this fell on Paget but, as a result, the teaching of surgery in the medical schools and universities improved and the standards of examining by the Colleges rose. Later, the board took on the duties of examining for the Navy and Army.

In 1856 he was elected an Associate of the Société de Biologie of Paris. There were only twenty associates from all over Europe and in the election he beat Rokitansky to the position. On 15 April he was elected a Corresponding Member of the Medico-Chirurgical Society of Edinburgh and in December an Honorary Member of the Philosophical Society of Cambridge. This was also the first year in which his income was greater than his expenses.

During 1856 he was concerned for his father's health and in letter to his brother, George, he wondered whether it would be improved by doubling his daily one to two glasses of port wine. Samuel died in April 1857 and James wrote to his brother, George; "This morning brought me the account of our father's death; a solemn, rather than a sad, event; for it would be to wish that we were immortal upon earth, if we were to desire to die otherwise than he had died. He outlived all his griefs: and was, at last, hardly sensible of earthly joy; but it may be a source of great happiness to us that, so long as he could think, he thought happily of us, and that we have been enabled to assist in making the end of his life here serene and free from cares of this world."

So ended the life of a man who had started with very little but through his hard work, initiatives and dedication had built up several successful businesses, had built a mansion on South Quay and had fathered a large family. He had educated and looked after his children and, with his wife, had encouraged them to follow his work ethic and his belief in God. Unfortunately, he appears to have overstretched himself financially, the contracts with the Royal Navy became fewer as the Navy used Yarmouth less and the brewery lost money. As a result, he was paying large sums of money in interest to his business partner, Dawson Turner, which he could not sustain, and he ended up selling his home and all his possessions. It was only the devotion of his sons in paying off his creditors that prevented him from suffering further humiliation.

Following their father's death Patty and Kate, his two daughters, moved to Kirstead, Norfolk to live with and look after their youngest brother Alfred who was unmarried and the rector of the parish. He had previously been a schoolmaster at Shrewsbury. Kirstead is approximately 15 miles southwest of Yarmouth and had about 55 homes and a population of approximately 250 people in the 1850s. Alfred died in 1862 and the two sisters moved to a cottage in Pinner, Middlesex which they shared with Elsie, one of the daughters of their eldest brother, Frederick, who had emigrated to Switzerland.

In May 1857 he gave the Royal Society's Croonian Lecture which had been established by William Croone (1633-16684), one of the original Fellows of the Society. Although he had planned in his will to give this lecture to the Royal Society and another to the Royal College of Physicians he had not endowed them and this was done subsequently by his widow. The one to the Royal Society is regarded as the premier lecture in Biological Sciences, was a great honour for Paget and his title was 'On the Cause of the Rhythmic Motion of the Heart'. He started by referring to the heart beat of the frog with its nerve centres within the muscle. He covered many examples of rhythm in both animals and plants and drew the conclusion that this results from the rhythmical process of nutrition and refers to the recurrence of thirst and hunger, the daily rise and fall of temperature and the sleeping and waking of animals and plants. He referred to maturity and death and this was particularly poignant as it was just a month since his father had died. His wide ranging coverage about plants and animals and how they worked indicated the extent of his knowledge and the lecture was even more impressive in that he delivered it without notes.

By this time his private practice was thriving but he was still helping to pay off his father's creditors. He wrote to his brother George on 23 September 1857: "Thank God I have been able to save enough of this payment without cutting into my October earnings. It is a novel sensation, and a very agreeable one, to find my income surpass my expenses, even though the surplus is thus quickly swept away. The good result of this year is entirely due to increase of practice and I am most thankful to say that the increase is of a kind which I may reasonably hope to go on. Here is my cheque - for the largest sum I ever drew for any purpose of my own - sent with a mixture of regret that it will sweep away all my savings, and of gladness that I have been enabled to save so much. God help us still to obey His own command to owe no man anything but love. For the January payment, I must look chiefly to my October earnings. I will work hard to meet it: and if (D.V.) I succeed, I'll keep a very jolly birthday on the 11th."

The lease on his house in Henrietta Street expired in 1858 and he moved to 1 Harewood Place, Hanover Square at the end of January. The cost of this was very much more, but his income could afford it and his expanding family benefitted from the extra space. Nevertheless, he was concerned that if anything should happen to him his family would be in severe financial difficulty.

The house was just off Oxford Street and was approached from Hanover Square. It was quiet, as there was no passing traffic, and he considered it well placed for his private practice. On the ground floor his study and the dining room were either side of a wide hall. His study was spartanly furnished with straight backed chairs and a horsehair sofa. There was no surgical couch, screen nor mirror. The walls were covered with books and portraits with prime places being given to John Hunter, Percival Pott, Abernethy, Lawrence and Queen Victoria. On the first floor were the drawing room and the 'school room'.

Although 1 Harewood Place was a grand house, life within it was simple and money was not spent needlessly. Before he had a carriage he would usually walk to the hospital and often used to read as he went along until one day he knocked over a small child he had not seen. On Sundays he would sometimes take some of his children to the hospital and take them round a few of the wards.

He would normally see twenty or more private patients at his home in the morning. During a consultation he would normally stand and be rather formal. He exchanged few words with the patient although he would speak freely to the doctor if one accompanied the patient. Stephen, his son, quotes an example when he and the patient, a Yorkshireman, were equally brief in their exchanges. On coming into the room the man thrust out his lip and said "What's that?" "That's cancer" Paget replied. "And what's to be done about it?" "Cut it out." "What's your fee?" "Two guineas." "You must make a deal of money at that rate." That was the end of the consultation.

Although he was increasingly busy with his private patients he never let them interfere with his duties to his hospital patients. Adam Young, his last house surgeon, said "I do not recollect his ever allowing his private work to interfere with keeping his appointments at the hospital; I know of many occasions he had infinite trouble in doing so. ......He expected us to take the greatest pains with all the details of our work, and he held the House-surgeon personally responsible for the state of the Wards and the condition of the patients. He used to preach to us, on all and every occasion, the importance of absolute, painstaking, cleanliness in the treatment of surgical injuries; and, of as much importance, the gentle handling of wounds." The care and the gentleness with which he showed his patients was also recorded by Mr. Fairbank, one of his last four dressers: "His tenderness to the patients was a lesson to us all: when he had to say an unpleasant thing to a patient, his gentle sympathetic manner took out much of the sting and sorrow. If he had a poor patient leaving the Hospital, who was in want, I have seen Paget go back, after we were supposed to have gone away, and give him a handful of silver, never troubling to see how much there was."

Although he appears to have been a very reasonable surgeon his reputation was built on his ability to make diagnoses and to give sound advice as to the best management for the condition presented. It was said that if you wanted to know what was wrong with you should go to Paget and then go to Fergusson to have it removed. Sir William Fergusson was senior surgeon at King's College Hospital and following his death Paget succeeded him as Sergeant Surgeon to Queen Victoria. Paget called him the "greatest master of the art, the greatest practical surgeon of our time" in his Hunterian Oration which he delivered in February 1877, three days after Fergusson's death.

Some younger surgeons felt it was unfair to them that he

charged some patients reduced fees or none at all. However, this is a long established custom among many consultants and Paget would not have wanted to act differently from them.

As he grew older he socialised more but would never go out more than three evenings in the week. He belonged to a number of clubs but would not attend all their meetings. Lord Aldenham, President of the Club of Nobody's Friends, says this of him "it was always a pleasure to hear him speak. His pleasant voice, his well-chosen words, however sudden or unexpected the call upon him - never saying too much, but always saying much in few words - gave an example to all of us. No man more zealously than he maintained and enforced the leading principle of our Society, which is 'Devotion to Church and King'."

One private dinner party he enjoyed was the Octave hosted by Sir Henry Thompson (1820-1904), Professor of Surgery at University College Hospital who had a special interest in urological surgery. These dinners were for eight distinguished men plus the host and guest of honour which he held at his home 35 Wimpole Street. The dinner started at 8pm and consisted of eight courses and eight different wines. One of these dinners was captured in an oil painting by Joseph Solomon, RA in 1897 in which a very elderly looking Paget is seen sitting to the right of Sir Henry Thompson who has Ernest Hart, the editor of the British Medical Journal, sitting on his left. Both Paget and Thompson had their portraits painted by John Everett Millais.

Octavian Dinner Party. Painting by Joseph Solomon, RA in 1897. Paget is second from left of portrait.
(Wellcome Library, London).

In the evenings he would sometimes read aloud the works of Dickens, Tennyson and Wilkie Collins or sing while his wife played the piano. Occasionally they would sing together. At other times he would demonstrate slides under the microscope to his children.

Every evening after dinner, or after returning from a function, he would place his desk on the dining table and would occupy no more than two and a half feet of it. This was sufficient for his desk, papers, letters and a glass of wine. He would sometimes praise the music but would continue writing until 10 o'clock when he would read prayers. After this he would continue writing until midnight when he would send his letters to the post. He would continue further writing or reading until 1 or 2 in the morning.

Lydia, his wife, was always writing long letters to her children and others. She underestimated her abilities and spent much time helping the poor and needy. She was an accomplished musician and had studied at the Royal Academy of Music. She composed music and for some time in her early years was a music teacher.

In March 1858 he was appointed Surgeon Extraordinary to Queen Victoria. This came as a surprise to many of his colleagues but there was rejoicing in Yarmouth and the Mayor presented him with an address of congratulation from the Town Council. The following month he was elected a member of the Philosophical Club.

In May he had another bout of pneumonia and felt close to death. He made an excellent recovery then three of his children contracted scarlet fever in the autumn during a major epidemic in which many thousands died or were made invalids. To give thanks for their recovery, and his own from the peumonia, he had a memorial window made for his new home.

On 8 April 1859 he gave a lecture at the Royal Institution on 'The Chronometry of Life' which he had touched on in his Croonian Lecture. It deals with the time regulation and adjustments concerned with life and reproduction. He sent a copy of the lecture to Charles Darwin.

After sixteen years in post he resigned from the position of Lecturer in Physiology on 14 June 1859. He did this because his expanding private practice gave him little time to prepare for the lectures which took up nine hours each week. He felt unable to keep up to date as he had little time for reading and he knew few of the students. He would loose the £300 which he received as a lecturer but this would be more than made up by private fees.

In 1860 he joined the Senate of London University and was appointed to examine candidates for the Army Medical Service.

He succumbed to another attack of pneumonia in February 1861. On 3 April he became senior Assistant Surgeon by the promotion of Mr. Wormald to Surgeon following the resignation of Mr. Lloyd. On 24 July, at the age of 47, he became one of the Surgeons of St. Bartholomew's after Mr. Stanley resigned. The following month he had his first real holiday since 1844 and took his wife and daughter to North Wales for three weeks. He thoroughly enjoyed the freedom of his holiday and remarked that never again would he have to be persuaded to take another.

In 1862 he paid the final instalment of his father's debts and even searched for those people who had not sent in a claim. At least one he repaid along with interest.

He replaced Mr. Lloyd as Surgeon to Christ's Hospital on 23

January 1862 and in the summer gave an address to the British Medical Association 'On the treatment of patients after surgical operations'. In 1863 he was appointed Surgeon-in-Ordinary to the Prince of Wales and the second edition of his Lectures on Surgical Pathology was published after considerable help in revising them by Sir William Turner. He was invited to give the Introductory Address to the medical students on 1 October 1863. He reminded them that being a member of the medical profession brought with it special responsibilities: not to look after their own interests but especially those of "God and man". It was so important for them to remember that they would be looking after the lives and welfare of their fellow men. He stressed the importance of learning how to learn and that should start at medical school. If they did not do so then they would not make the best use of their experiences. He advised them not to appear clever but to strive to be wise. He warned them against "the apparent success of dishonesty" for the "supply of rogues is duly proportional to that of fools." He felt that "until there is a widespread teaching in natural science, there probably will always be much success in quackery." In his own life he had worked hard and strived for success and he ended his talk by saying "The burden of my address is work, lifelong work. And so it is, and so it must be; there is no success without it, no happiness without it. A kind of success, indeed, there is without it - the getting of money without honour - and to that there are many ways; but we do not teach that here." This neatly sums up his whole philosophy of life; of how he had devoted his life to learning and looking after his patients and without doing so there would have been no rewards.

Honours from abroad continued and on 6 January 1864 he was elected an Associate of the Société de Chirurgie (He had been made a Corresponding Member of the Society on 31 December 1856) and on 1 February a Member of the Accademia de' Quiriti di Roma. Previously he had been elected a Foreign Associate of the Société de Biologie on 19 April 1856.

He had yet another bout of pneumonia in January 1865 and

in July was elected to the Council of the Royal College of Surgeons. In October he gave the Inaugural Address at Leeds School of Medicine to mark the opening of its new buildings. He was also appointed Joint Lecturer in Surgery at St. Bartholomew's along with Mr. Holmes Coote. In a letter to Sir William Turner, who had recently been appointed Professor of Anatomy at Edinburgh, he says that his surgical class is the largest in London and larger than it has been at St. Bartholomew's for twenty years.

Occasionally he would be invited to see patients outside London. Sometimes he would complain about the poor payment received which made it not worthwhile, especially as on his return to London he had to catch up on so much of his normal work. On other occasions the complexity or the interest of the condition made the trip worthwhile. However, the journey could be difficult and trying as he described in a letter to his wife on 31 July 1866 "My long journey was not a very pleasant one - for I had to be driven 12 miles beyond Sheffield, over a rather bad road, during pelting rain and a high wind, between 3 and 5 a.m."

8

HOLIDAYS AND HONOURS

Much of Paget's early life was devoted to work and rarely did he take time off. This was made necessary by lack of money and his constant desire to learn and improve himself. His first real holiday was in August 1861 went he went to North Wales for three weeks. He enjoyed the freedom so much that he planned to have a holiday every year. Some of these were associated with work. For example, he spent August and September 1867 attending to the Princess of Wales at Wiesbaden during her long illness. It enabled him to enjoy travel to other towns and cities in Germany as well as to appreciate the beauty of the Rhine. It also gave him the opportunity of mixing with European medical men and associations, and on one occasion he went to Frankfurt to the meeting of the Association of Doctors and Nature-Observers. Four hundred people were present and he had the seat of honour next to the President of the Association.

1868 was the first time the family took a holiday together and this became a regular feature and looked forward to by all concerned. However, Paget insisted that it had to involve education. Six days a week, everyone was expected to spend the whole morning reading and to do further reading in the evening making a total of four to six hours daily. The topics depended upon the age and ability of the children but included law, divinity, logic, Greek and Latin. Some evenings were spent listening to and making music. Paget would spend the morning writing letters or lectures. In the afternoon the party would spend the time on long expeditions in the open countryside, walking and driving. On some occasions the whole day would be spent on an expedition when they might cover 20 miles. They would exist on local food bought at inns and the young men would go for a swim if there was the opportunity. Paget relished these occasions to be free of his work and responsibilities at home and enjoyed the most simplest of activities of walking, talking or sleeping out in the open air. However, the main pleasure was being with his wife and children and devoting himself to their education, welfare and pleasure.

James Paget. Signed sketch by Charles Holl based on drawing by George Richmond in 1867.

Paget loved exploring and seeing the countryside, new towns and cities. He enjoyed concerts, pictures, visiting churches and other fine buildings. In later life he spent many hours wandering around and appreciating the many old buildings and sites of the city of London. This love and appreciation of art he dates to the experiences he had in his youth at the house on South Quay. He relished the opportunities to visit such places as Munich, Florence and Venice and to listen to great music by such as Bach, Leo and Purcell. Frequently he referred in various letters to the beauty of different flowers and plants in his home.

Back at home honours continued to be bestowed upon him and on 5 August 1868 he was awarded the honorary degree of D.C.L. of Oxford University alongside Sir Charles Locock, Sir William Jenner, Dr. Haughton, Sir William Gull, Sir John Simon and Mr. Syme. The previous day Mr. Syme and he had been awarded the honorary degree of MD of the University of Bonn and it is of interest that the citation puts his work as a pathologist above that as a surgeon.

In September he holidayed at Ballater near Balmoral and on one occasion he joined the Prince of Wales hunting for deer. He was interested in the way in which the animals were tracked but did not participate in the shooting. He appeared to have little interest in animals and this extended to his horses and other animals at his home. Nevertheless he had a certain affection for the Russian wolfhound he was given by the Princess of Wales.

He was appointed a member of the Royal Sanitary Commission in April 1869 and in August took his family holiday at Wildbad where he spent some time looking after the Princess of Wales. There were eleven people in the party. He thought Wildbad was very similar to Scotland. He was very unimpressed with the decadence of Baden Baden where there was a great deal of gambling for very high stakes, the ladies were very expensively dressed and the men "looked like fools or rogues".

As President of the Clinical Society of London he gave the first address of the session on the importance of clinical work and that it deserved to be called a science in its own right.

Throughout his professional life Paget was always interested in medical education and he investigated what happened to over one thousand of his medical students up to fifteen years after they entered medical school. He did this work with Mr. Callender and Sir Thomas Smith and it was published in the St. Bartholomew's Hospital Reports in 1869 as 'What becomes of Medical Students'. He compared the outcomes with his views of them as students and concluded that a man is, in practice, what he was as a student. The results showed:

    23 achieved distinguished success
    66 achieved considerable success
  507 achieved fair success
  124 achieved very limited success
    56 failed entirely
    96 left the profession
    87 died within twelve years of practice
    41 died during pupillage, 17 of tuberculosis.

Medicine then was a hazardous occupation as is indicated by the fact that four of the students died of fever caught in the hospital and twenty-one who died in practice succumbed from 'diseases incurred in their duties'. One was hung for the murder of a friend. The paper supported Paget's long held view that, irrespective of what happened after qualifying, the success or failure of the person was defined by how he performed as a student. "Nothing appears more certain than that the personal character, the very nature, the will, of each student has far greater force in determining his career than any helps or hindrances whatever. All my recollections would lead me to tell that every student may draw from his daily life a very likely forecast of his life in practice; for it will depend on himself a hundredfold more than on circumstances."

In 1870 the third edition of the Lectures on Surgical Pathology was published with the help of Sir William Turner. At the time, Paget felt that in future it should be replaced by a volume of Clinical Lectures on various subjects.

The commonest cause of death in hospitals at this time was infection and 25-50% of patients having operations succumbed from it. The cause was unknown until the work of Pasteur although the Hungarian obstetrician, Ignaz Semmelweiss (1818-1865), had studied the problem of puerperal fever - infections developing in ladies after childbirth. Puerperal fever was extremely common with a mortality of 10-35% and he noticed that the mortality rate was three times greater in the doctors' wards than in the midwives' wards. In 1847 his friend, Jakob Kolletschka, died after being cut by a scalpel while performing a postmortem and the autopsy on him showed a similar appearance to that found in women dying from puerperal fever.

He thought that 'cadaverous particles' were transferred to the pregnant ladies on the hands of doctors coming from the postmortem room and he dramatically reduced the incidence of the disease by insisting that everyone in the labour wards washed their hands in a solution of chlorinated lime before examining a patient. This brought the mortality rate down to 1%.

Unfortunately, Semmelweiss's work was disbelieved by the medical profession as it was thought that disease resulted from an imbalance of the 'four humours' in the body; the main treatment for which was blood letting. When his position at the Vienna Lying-in Hospital came up for renewal he was not reappointed. Eventually he became Professor of Obstetrics at the University of Pest where again he showed the dramatic decline in mortality by instituting hand washing with chlorine. Nevertheless, his results were ignored, his behaviour became increasingly odd and he was admitted to a mental asylum in 1865 where he died fourteen days later. The value of his work was only appreciated after the 'germ theory' proposed by Louis Pasteur (1822-1895). He showed that fermentation was caused by micro-organisms and he demonstrated with boiled broths that by putting a filter in the entrance to the container fermentation was prevented. Similarly, vessels which had a long spiral neck and no filter protected the broth from contamination. He and Claude Bernard demonstrated that heating milk would kill off bacteria and moulds and this process became known as pasteurization. This work led him to believe that micro-organisms might cause disease in animals and humans and this was taken a stage further by Lister who devised methods of preventing bacteria from contaminating wounds.

Joseph Lister (1827-1912) was born in Upton, Essex to a Quaker family and his father had pioneered advances in the microscope. He did his medical training at University College, London after initially obtaining a degree in Botany. He moved to Edinburgh Royal Infirmary and in 1854 he became first assistant to James Syme (1799-1870), Professor of Surgery, whose daughter he later married. At the time, surgeons operated in the clothes they wore on the streets and in the wards and there was no attempt to wash hands. It was thought that wounds became infected due to exposure to bad air, so called miasma, and to deal with this wards were built with high ceilings and large windows.

Lister was appointed Professor of Surgery at Glasgow University and while there he became aware of Pasteur's work showing that infection was caused by micro-organisms and suggesting that they could be eliminated by filtration, heat or chemicals. Lister decided to use carbolic acid which had been used to reduce the smell in the sewers. He had his instruments, dressings and wounds sprayed in carbolic acid. In August 1865 an eleven year old boy was brought to the hospital with a compound fracture of his leg. Such an injury normally resulted in severe infection and the standard treatment was an amputation to try to prevent this. Lister decided to treat the wound with lint soaked in carbolic acid and when he changed the dressing four days later there was no evidence of infection. The dressings were continued and by six weeks the fractured bone had healed. He reported the results in the Lancet and on 9 August 1867 he read a paper at a meeting of the British Medical Association in Dublin entitled 'Antiseptic Principle of the Practice of Surgery'. In 1869 he became Professor of Surgery in Edinburgh, in succession to Syme, and later he moved to London to become Professor of Surgery at King's College Hospital. He was elevated to the House of Lords in 1897 and was one of the original twelve members of the Order of Merit which was established in 1902.

Like so many medical advances it took time for the importance of Lister's work to be appreciated and to be put into practice. Certainly, it took sometime before Paget was convinced. In February 1871 Paget developed blood poisoning after carrying out a postmortem examination. Mr. Bloxam, surgical registrar at St. Bartholomew's, was his assistant who also became dangerously ill for a number of weeks. Paget reported his illness in the Lancet in 1871 and noted that he developed some small pustules on his hands which he thought "were only local effects of the simply irritant fluids of the body, or of the carbolic acid oil, with which I had uselessly though thoroughly rubbed my hands before beginning my part of the examination." He developed abscesses in his neck and left arm pit which were drained. He became extremely unwell coming close to death and at one stage requested consultations with ten of the leading medical authorities. He notes that Sir William Lawrence used to say that he knew of no-one surviving who had had more than seven consultations yet he, Paget, had been attended by ten eminent clinicians. "In this multitude of counsellors was safety."

In the paper he explains that he feels that the body builds up immunity to the poisons of the dissecting room and during the early part of his career he spent much of each day in the dissecting rooms. In more recent times he rarely went there and, if he did, he was there as an observer and so had lost his immunity and became prone to developing the severe infection which nearly took his life.

In this Lancet paper he clearly feels that carbolic acid is of no value and may have caused the pustules on his hands. Lister wrote a private letter to his friend Paget extolling the virtues of carbolic acid in preventing infection before writing in a similar vein to the Lancet.

9

RETIREMENT FROM ST. BARTHOLOMEW'S

As a result of this severe infection Paget decided to reduce his responsibilities and resign from St. Bartholomew's Hospital. On 4 July 1871 the Prince of Wales formally thanked him for all he had done for the hospital and we was appointed Consulting Surgeon. To retire from the hospital was a momentous decision and one which he must have found very difficult to make. The hospital had been part of his life for 37 years and he had visited it nearly every day. He had been a medical student, demonstrator, lecturer and surgeon as well as warden of the college overseeing the transformation of the medical school to it being one of the best in London. As a surgeon he had worked just as hard as he had during his days as a pathologist and he had built up an international reputation, was respected by his colleagues and the students were devoted to him.

Shortly after his retirement from the hospital he was appointed a baronet which he took great joy in but more for the benefit it would have for the medical profession and his children rather than himself. He took as his motto one in which he and his brothers had shared as children: 'Work itself is a pleasure'. This really sums up the way had had lived his life.

To mark his retirement, his colleagues and friends commissioned John Everett Millais to paint his portrait and this was presented to him in June 1873. Millais (1829-1896) was a prolific and fashionable painter who had founded the Pre-Raphaelite Brotherhood in 1848 with William Holden Hunt and Dante Gabriel Rossetti. He is well known for his paintings of Bubbles, The Boyhood of Raleigh and Ophelia and later painted, among many others, Disraeli, Gladstone and Darwin. Millais made sketches for the painting while Sir James lectured to the students. The portrait is rather sombre with him dressed in black clothes and looking rather solemn. Adam Young, his last house surgeon, wrote "The Millais portrait is a telling likeness of what he was in those days; but I think it shows signs of the dreadful illness he had just passed through; and there is a sadness in the expression which I don't recollect was usual with him; for he was about to give up his work at the Hospital, to which he was so passionately devoted, and all who were intimately acquainted with him know what a grief and trouble this was to him."

Portrait of Sir James Paget by John Millais

(© St. Bartholomew's Hospital Archives)

For many years the painting hung in the Great Hall at St. Bartholomew's but is now in a smaller room. An engraving of the portrait was made by Thomas Oldham Barlow (1824 - 1889) and copies were sold. Most had a print of Paget's Signature below the portrait and a few had original signatures of Millais, Barlow and Paget. The original engraving is in the National Portrait Gallery after it was presented to the Gallery in 1910 by two of Barlow's daughters.

A copy of the original Millais painting was commissioned by some of Paget's friends and presented to the Great Yarmouth Borough Council. The artist is unknown but it is a very good copy. It hung in the Great Yarmouth General Hospital, which he opened in 1888, until it closed in 1982. It is now on display in the James Paget University Hospital which was opened in December 1981.

Water colour and pencil sketch by medical student, Alexander Boswell(1853-1936). Drawn in 1874
(© St. Bartholomew's Hospital Archives)

He also resigned from his position as Surgeon to Christ's Hospital on 23 May 1871 and on 29 November the President of the Hospital, The Duke of Cambridge, thanked him for all the work he had done.

Towards the end of December he was called to Sandringham to see whether the Prince of Wales required surgery in the management of the typhoid fever from which he was suffering. He felt that surgery was not required and the Prince made an uncomplicated recovery.

In 1872 he was elected an Honorary Fellow of the Royal Society of Edinburgh and a Fellow of the Linnean Society. The Linnean Society was founded in 1788 and is named after the Swedish naturalist Carl Linnaeus (1707-1778) and today is the world's oldest active biological society.

In 1873 he was elected a member of Grillion's Club which had been founded as a dining club in 1812 by Stratford Cannning as a meeting place free from the violence of political controversy. The same year he was made an honorary member of the Medical Society of London which had been founded in 1773 by John Coakley Lettsom to be a meeting place for physicians, surgeons and apothecaries. In December 1773 he had another attack of pneumonia.

In 1874 he received the honorary degree of LL.D of Cambridge at the opening of the new Cavendish Laboratory. He was President of the Section of Surgery for the meeting of the British Medical Association held in Norwich and was elected an Associate of the College of Physicians of Philadelphia and a Corresponding Member of the Academy of Medicine of New York. In September and early October he visited Belgium and Holland, enjoying the scenery - some of which he said was reminiscent of Gorleston and Caister, two small towns near Yarmouth - walking and listening to music.

1874 was also the year in which he wrote the paper 'On Disease of the Mammary Areola Preceding Cancer of the Mammary Gland' for the St. Bartholomew's Hospital Reports. He described "about fifteen cases.... in age from 40-60 or more years" in which there was a rawness of the areola of the breast. In all patients a cancer developed in the breast within two years. He had operated on two of these patients but with disappointing results. He suggested that the irritation around the nipple was the cause of the development of the breast carcinoma. This is now known not to be the case. The tumour of the breast develops first either as an invasive cancer or as an extensive carcinoma in situ and it is thought that growth of these carcinoma in situ cells along the ducts then invade the epidermis of the nipple so causing the ulceration.

First page of paper on 'Disease of the Mammary Areola preceding Cancer of the Mammary Gland'

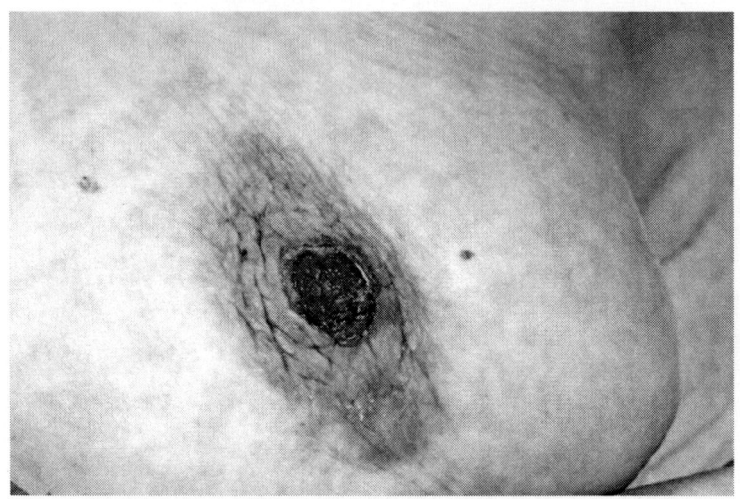

Nipple changes (Rawness) in patient with Paget's Disease of Nipple.

In the same paper he refers to a "persistent rawness of the glans penis, like a long-enduring balanitis, followed after more than a year's duration by a cancer of the substance of the glans." Under the microscope the large clear malignant cells (Called Paget cells) seen in the epidermis in Paget's disease of the nipple are also found in the glans penis. However, Paget did not give these microscopic descriptions in this article and in this he was not following his teaching of the importance of using the microscope to aid in diagnosis and in the understanding of disease. The reasons for this are probably that he was too busy with his private practice or that he no longer had easy access to a microscope. Two years later Henry Butlin, one of his previous house surgeons, described the microscopic appearances of two patients who had Paget's disease of the nipple.

In 1875 he was elected President of the Royal College of Surgeons of England following in the steps of another Great Yarmouth man, Sir Astley Cooper, who was President twice - in

1827 and 1836. The Secretary of the College then was Mr. Trimmer who said "He was a most active member of the Council, and a prominent member of its several important committees, and took a deep interest in all matters relating to the welfare of the College. He was chiefly instrumental in bringing about the change whereby separate examiners in Anatomy and Physiology were appointed to carry on the examinations in those subjects, in the place of the Court of examiners; and he was one of the most influential members of the Committee by whose help the scheme for the Conjoint Examinations by the Royal Colleges of Physicians and of Surgeons was brought to a successful issue. He was an excellent man of business, and always punctual in his attendance at meetings, and I never remember his having been absent, except through illness, from meetings of the Council. He was a most charming man with whom to transact business, being courteous to all with whom he came in contact, and ever ready to listen and give weight to the opinions of others who might differ from him. On his retirement from the Council, he still kept up his interest in College affairs, and apart from his attendance as a Trustee of the Hunterian Collection, he frequently paid me friendly visits to learn the last Collegiate news."

The obituary in the Times of January 1, 1900 said "In the Council of the College of Surgeons he exercised great influence, which was partly due to his inclination to be with the majority. He went with the tide to a considerable extent, and would seldom persevere in an opposition which seemed unlikely to be successful; not from the slightest inclination towards time-serving, but from genuine intellectual modesty, which led him to distrust his own judgement, and to think of the probability that others might understand the question at issue better than he did himself.... In questions of right, however, he admitted no compromise: and, both by precept and by example, he invariably upheld the highest standard of professional honour and integrity."

Group portrait of College Council 1884-85. Paget is 9th from left and Lister is 4th from right. Large portrait of John Hunter on the wall.
(Royal College of Surgeons)

During his term of office there was continuing debate about whether to have a Conjoint Board examination run by the Royal College of Surgeons of England and the Royal College of Physicians to enable students to qualify as doctors by awarding them diplomas in medicine and surgery. Paget supported the idea but it would be another ten years before the idea was adopted.

In the middle of the nineteenth century there was increasing interest in physiology which resulted in more experiments on animals to observe how organs worked and responded to various influences. It was thought that animals did not feel pain. As a physiology lecturer, Paget had illustrated his lectures with experiments on animals and as a leader of his profession as a surgeon it was inevitable that he would become involved in the debates about vivisection.

Vivisection, which became to mean experimenting on living animals, had been practiced for two thousand years but the outcry about it increased in the 1870s. One of its chief opponents was Frances Power Cope (1822-1904) who was an Irish writer, social reformer and a fighter for women's rights.

She arranged a form of marriage with Mary Lloyd, a sculptress, early in 1860 and lived with her until Mary's death.

Frances Power Cope set up the Victoria Street Society on 2 December 1875 and it was renamed the National Anti-Vivisection Society in October 1897. Soon it had some very influential supportors such as the Archbishop of York, the Earl of Shaftesbury and Tennyson. Robert Browning (1812-1889) wrote "I despise and abhor the pleas on behalf of that infamous practice, vivisection... I would rather submit to the worst of deaths, so far as pain goes, than have a single dog or cat tortured to death on the pretense of sparing me a twinge or two." Charles Dickens (1812-1870) supported the cause: "The necessity for these experiments I dispute. Man has no right to gratify an idle and purposeless curiosity through the practice of cruelty." Anna Sewell (1820-1877), born of Quaker parents in Great Yarmouth, indirectly supported the movement by writing 'Black Beauty' when she was aged 56, shortly before her death. This was the autobiography of a horse recounting the cruelty suffered by horses.

The Victoria Street Society received the support of Queen Victoria who arranged for a letter to be sent to Joseph Lister asking him for his support but in a long reply he failed to give his support. Most surgeons held the same view although Sir William Ferguson (1808-1877), President of the College of Surgeons in 1870, supported the anti-vivisectionists. The First Royal Commission on Vivisection was appointed in 1875 and Paget spoke in favour of the introduction of legislation to control vivisection. The initial Bill would have seriously handicapped the work of scientists and, following a meeting of Paget, Joseph Hooker and Burdon-Smith (Professor of Practical Physiology at University College London) with the Home Secretary, modifications were made. This led to the Cruelty to Animals Act 1876 which remained in force until it was replaced by the Animals (Scientific Procedures) Act 1986.

Although supporting legislation to control vivisection practices Paget was still a strong supporter of it as is shown in the article he wrote for the journal Nineteenth Century: "At the present time 20,000 persons are annually killed by venomous snakes in India. If the discovery of a remedy without experiments on animals would come later by, say, five years, than one made by their help, would it be nothing to have lost 100,000 lives? The case is worth considering because of an almost absurd consequence of the Vivisection Act. I may pay a rat-catcher to destroy all the rats in my house with any poison that he pleases; but I may not myself, unless with a licence from the home Secretary, poison them with snake-poison, not, without an additional certificate, try to keep them alive after it."

To counter the activities of the anti-vivisectionists the Association for the Advancement of Medicine by Research was founded and held its first meeting at the Royal College of Physicians in May 1882 when the President of the College, Sir William Gull, was elected President of the new organisation. Paget was elected Vice-President and some years later his son, Stephen, was Secretary of the Association for the Advancement of Medicine by Research.

In 1875 Paget was President not only of the College of Surgeons but also of the Royal Medico-Chirurgical Society which had branched off from the Medical Society of London in 1805 in response to the autocratic style of Sir William Saunders who was President from 1786 until 1808. The Royal Medico-Chirurgical Society became the Royal Society of Medicine in 1907 by merging with the Pathological Society of London, the Epidemiological Society of London and some other organisations.

1875 saw the publication of his 'Clinical Lectures and Essays' which had been edited by his colleague Howard Marsh. This contained articles on gout, dissection wounds, strangulated hernias, the risks of operations, typhoid fever and the nervous mimicry of disease. Throughout there was advice to students as in the section on 'the calamities of surgery'. "One continually hears it said, 'I did my best; but these things will happen'; and yet what a man has called 'doing his best' was not doing so well as he had done before, or so well as he will do next time. Let me warn you against this. Men constantly say, 'These things have happened to better men: they have happened to this or that person of distinction; so I need not be surprised at having them.' There is no more miserable or false plea than this. But there are some people who seem to have a happy art of forgetting all their failures, and remembering nothing but their successes, and, as I have watched such men in professional life, years have always made them worse instead of better surgeons. They seem to have a faculty of reckoning all failures as little, and all successes as big; they make their brains like sieves, and they run all the little things through, and retain all the big ones which they suppose to be their successes; and a very mischievous heap of rubbish it is that they retain."

At the beginning of 1876 the magazine 'Vanity Fair' published a caricature of him by Spy. On the 13 February he writes to his son Stephen "I hope you have seen 'Vanity Fair'. The face seems to be fairly like, the figure absurdly unlike." The adjoining article suggests that he had never given a lecture, written a book or worked in a hospital. Paget says he found the whole article and drawing amusing and no-one could have laughed at it as much as he did.

Sir James Paget. Chromolithograph by Spy
(Wellcome Library, London)

He was appointed to represent the Royal College of Surgeons on the General Medical Council on 13 July 1876 and continued on the Council until 1881. The Council had been established following the Medical Act of 1858 which stated 'it is expedient that Persons requiring Medical Aid should be enabled to distinguish qualified from unqualified Practitioners'. Before this time doctors had received licenses to practice from the church and its bishops and the Royal College of Physicians had overseen the work of Physicians in London. Nevertheless many people could set themselves up as medical practitioners without any worthwhile qualifications or any means of regulation. Paget was elected to the Finance and Executive Committees of the Council in May 1877 and continued on them until his retirement from the Council in June 1881. Although he was involved in many discussions and activities by the Council he did not enjoy the work and felt the Council was not very effective. He had written to his brother, George, on 12 June, which was before his appointment, "I dislike the kind of work; it distresses me, costs me huge labour, and keeps me always self-discontented." He was hoping that after he had finished being President of the College he would be able to devote more of his time "to scientific work, some recreation and self-cultivation." His experiences on the Council confirmed his worse fears in that little seemed to be accomplished. On 27 March 1879, he wrote to his brother, George, "We sat for 8 days, and on 6 of them decided to do nothing."

In spite of his commitments to the College of Surgeons, the Medical-Chirurgical Society, the General Medical Council and his private patients he managed to produce his paper 'On a form of chronic inflammation of the bones (osteitis deformans)' which he presented to the Medico-Chirurgical Society on 14 November 1876. He reported five patients with abnormalities of their bones which had not been previously described. One patient he had followed for twenty years since he first met him in 1854 at the age of forty-six years of age. At that time the patient complained of aches and pains in his legs and Paget noted that the left tibia and femur were deformed and enlarged. Paget did not know what was the cause and over the years noted that similar changes appeared in the right leg and the patient's skull became enlarged so that he had to buy larger and larger hats. He began to stoop, he lost four inches in height but his health remained good. Twenty years after Paget first met him a rapidly growing mass appeared in his left forearm and within two months he died.

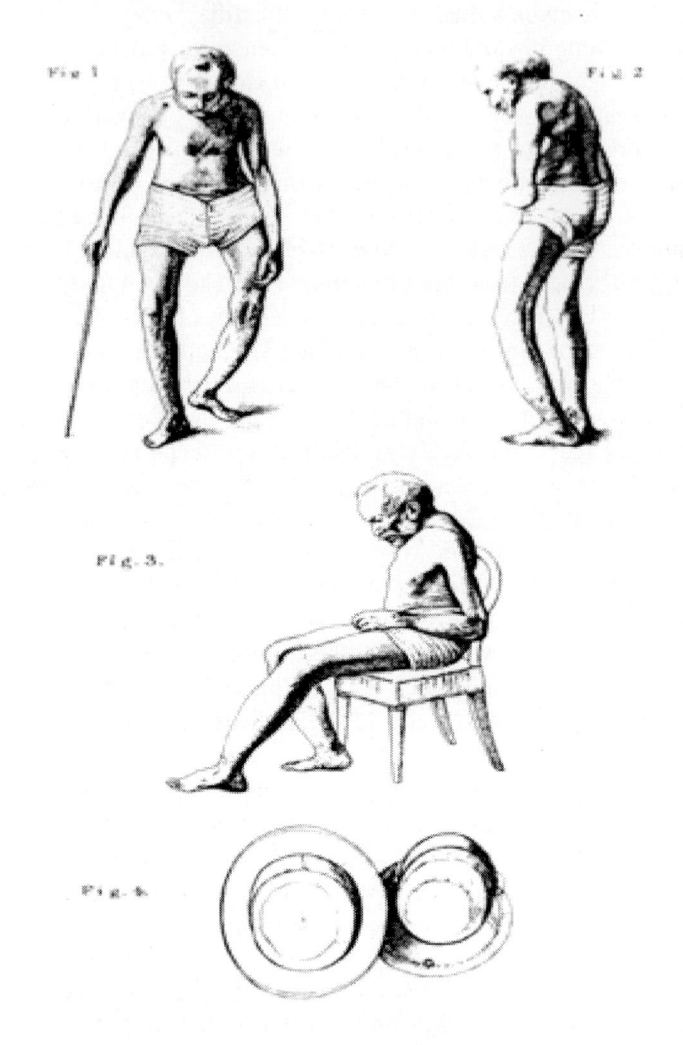

Drawings of one of his early patients showing bowing of his legs, large skull and hat size increasing from 1841 (on right) to 1876
(Royal College of Surgeons)

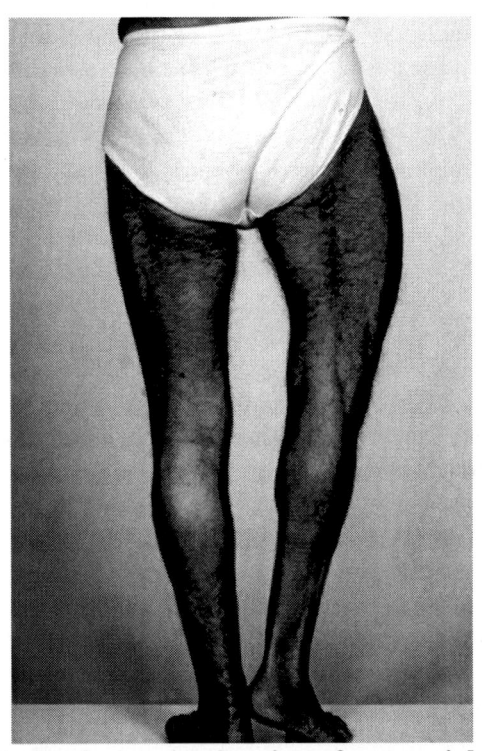

Photograph showing bowing of upper right leg

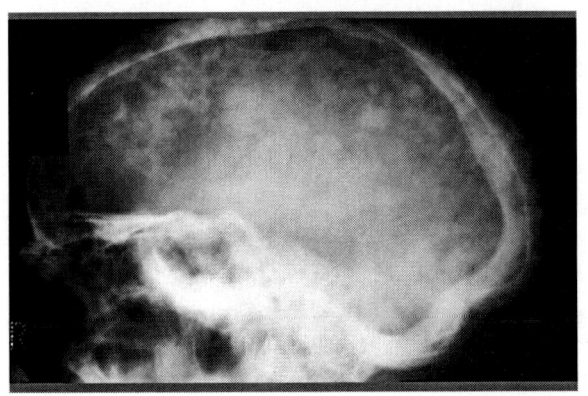

Xray showing thickening thickening and increased density of skull

The postmortem confirmed that the mass was a malignant tumour which had spread to the chest and skull. In this paper Paget included the results of microscopic studies which he had failed to do in his paper 'On Disease of the Mammary Areola Preceding Cancer of the Mammary Gland'. Microscopy of the palpable abnormal bones showed a very odd appearance. In a normal bone the bone cells are being constantly removed and laid down in response to the stresses on them. In this patient the remodelling of the bone appeared out of control resulting in the bones becoming thickened and weak so that they bent under the weight of the body. Paget thought that this was an inflammatory response so named the condition osteitis deformans. The microscopic studies, and probably the postmortem, were carried out by Henry Butlin who had been Paget's house surgeon and at the time was surgical registrar at St. Bartholomew's. Paget noted that three of his five patients developed bone tumours but subsequent studies show that malignancy is a rare complication of this disease. Although Paget was the first to describe this condition, examination of Egyptian skeletons which are several thousand years old show that it existed then. Again we see the results of Paget's observations and meticulous note taking.

He was elected an Honorary Member of the Odontological Society of Great Britain in December 1876 and in September had a wonderful holiday in Italy. During that time he was considering whether he should give up operating and just continue with consultations.

He delivered his Hunterian Oration on 13 February 1877. This is a very prestigious occasion for any surgeon but few could have had such a distinguished audience as among the guests were the Prince of Wales, Mr. Gladstone, the Duke of Argyle, the Duke of Westminster, Dean Stanley, Lord Acton, Mr. Huxley and many of the leading physicians and surgeons of the day. Paget's three sons were also present. Much of his lecture was devoted to the influence of Hunter on surgery. Before this time surgeons were subservient to physicians who had come from the ranks of the gentry, been better educated and had taught surgeons their anatomy. As a result of Hunter's influence, surgeons became the chief anatomists, and were well versed in pathology and anatomy. They were also accepted in higher society.

He pointed out that although Hunter had few friends, was prone to tantrums and appeared to be rather simple, his success was the result of his scientific studies. Paget's conclusion was 'that if we desire to maintain the rank of gentlemen, to hold this highest prize of our profession, we must do so by the highest scientific culture to which we can attain. And to this we are bound, not by our own advancement alone, but by every motive of the plainest duty."

In recounting details of Hunter's successes it is noteworthy how much of Paget's life had followed similar lines. His student days had started in poverty, he had studied and developed the basic sciences of anatomy, pathology and physiology and gone on to become a highly successful teacher and surgeon where he was accepted among the elite of society, many of whom were his friends.

At the dinner afterwards Mr. Gladstone (1809-1898) who had served the first of his four terms as Prime Minister from 1868 to 1874 proposed Paget's health in a rather long speech. In reply Paget said "There is only one way in which it may be possible to surpass Mr. Gladstone as an orator, and that way I will proceed to put in practice. You all know that, although speech may be silvern, silence is golden. You shall have the gold." With that he sat down. A few days later Paget received a letter from Dean Church recounting that Gladstone had described the Hunterian Oration as "a unique work of art in its kind, a 'miracle of compression'."

Three days before Paget gave his Hunterian Oration, Sir William Fergusson (1808-1877) had died. Fergusson was born in Scotland and became a fellow of the College of Surgeons of Edinburgh in 1829. He spent many hours dissecting and was elected surgeon to Edinburgh Royal Infirmary in 1836. In 1840 he was appointed Professor of Surgery at King's College Hospital, London. He became one of the most accomplished surgeons in London with great technical skill and was appointed Surgeon Extraordinary to Queen Victoria in 1855 and her Sergeant-Surgeon in 1867. Following Fergusson's death Paget was elected in his place as Sergeant Surgeon to Queen Victoria.

In February 1877 Paget was elected an Honorary Member of the American Academy of Arts and Sciences. His summer holiday was spent in Gloucestershire so he could be near his elder daughter who had married the Reverend H.L. Thompson, rector of Iron Acton, Gloucestershire who was later vicar of St. Mary's, Oxford. This is the University Church and the largest parish church in Oxford. On 27 November 1877, he presented his paper on 'Cases of Branchial Fistulae in the External Ears'.

10

WINDING DOWN

In 1877, after a great deal of thought and discussion with his brother George, he decided to give up most of his operating although he continued operating on small cases. The reasons were that he was nearly 65 years of age, the age that surgeons had to retire at St. Bartholomew's and other major hospitals, and he was concerned that poor sight and decreasing dexterity might result in him making a surgical error. His consulting practice did not diminish. On the contrary, he was in even greater demand, not only in London but around the country. Here the rapidly expanding railway network was a great help. He enjoyed the journeys as it enabled him to view the countryside and to keep up to date with his writing and reading. He seems to have been well paid for these excursions out of London.

About this time there was increasing discussion about the admission of women into the Medical Profession. In 1878 he had already met and had conversations with Mrs. Scharlieb, MD, who wanted to have a degree from the University of London. Because of religious practices in India and the Far East it was difficult for medical men to attend on well-born ladies and Sir James appreciated the problem, although he would not actively support her cause. In 1880 he was involved in the debate whether to allow women doctors from abroad to attend the International Medical Congress in London. He was slightly in favour of admitting them but was aware that the majority of British doctors would be against. He had also heard poor reports about a number of women doctors from Zurich and America which made him in favour of excluding women from the meeting. He felt it would cause a row but a smaller one than if they were admitted.

Sir James Paget. Photograph taken in 1881 by G. Jerrard.
(Wellcome Library, London)

In August 1880 he was President of the Section of Pathology at the British Medical Association meeting in Cambridge where his brother, George, was Regius Professor of Physic. His Presidential Address was entitled 'Elemental Pathology' which took him back to his teens when he was studying the flora in and around Yarmouth. It dealt with diseases and injuries affecting plants and trees and was based on his observations during his holidays, visits to the country and to Kew and Richmond. He was particularly interested in gall formation and felt that the process was similar to inflammatory changes due to recurrent irritation seen in animals. He thought that the study of degeneration, repair, inflammation, necrosis, hypertrophy, atrophy, tumour formation etc. in plants would help in the understanding of similar processes in animals and humans. The paper was published and he sent a copy of it to Charles Darwin who replied by saying "It is a surprising thought that the diseases of plants should illustrate human pathology." At the same meeting he also contributed a paper entitled ' Suggestions for the making of Pathological Catalogues'.

1881 was a particularly busy year for him and saw the culmination of two years work in preparation for the International Medical Congress in August. He was elected President and over three thousand doctors from all over the world attended. Among the others on the main organising committee were Sir William Jenner, Sir William Gull, Sir Risdon Bennett and Prof. (Later Lord) Lister.

Paget gave the Inaugural Address in the presence of the Prince of Wales, the Crown Prince of Germany, the Archbishop of York, the Cardinal Archbishop of Westminster, the Bishop of London, Pasteur, Virchow, Koch, Langenbeck, Charcot and many other celebrities. The Congress was held in many venues in London: The College of Physicians, the Royal Institution, the Royal Academy, the School of Practical Geology, the Royal Society and in several other places. Receptions were held at the South Kensington Museum, the Guildhall and the College of Surgeons and throughout the Congress he kept open house and entertained a large number of delegates at Harewood Place.

Stephen Paget gave some idea of the hospitality provided by the Paget's at Harewood Place: "He kept open house all the week, and three times a day entertained a large party of the members of the Congress. The house from morning to night was in a whirl of excitement, but it never lost its feeling of home. The incessant hospitality, the confusion of tongues, the coming and going of all the masters of medicine and surgery with their disciples, the meeting of H.R.H. the Prince of Wales and H.I.H. the Crown Prince of Germany with Darwin, Pasteur, Virchow, Huxley, Tyndall, and other great personages - all these festivities were still 'at home'; he could not easily imagine hospitality anywhere else: and the house, somehow, got through the work."

At the end of the Congress he was presented with an illuminated address which is in the Royal College of Surgeons of England. It says "At the concluding General Meeting of the International Congress in London, August 9th 1881, it was proposed by Professor Charcot, Seconded by Professor

Donders, and carried by acclamation; That the best thanks of the International Medical Congress be tendered to Sir James Paget. Bart., who with singular ability, assiduity and courtesy has presided over its seventh session in London from the second to the ninth of August, 1881; and who has powerfully contributed to the success of its objects by his high character, his dignified bearing and his eloquence. Signed William MacCormac. Hon. Sec Gen."

To end the Congress a dinner for 1,200 was held at the Crystal Palace which ended with a fireworks display.

The Congress had fifteen sections, which provided 119 sectional meetings, many general meetings as well as multiple social activities. The Transactions of the Congress were published later that year in four volumes covering 2,592 pages with 180 illustrations.

The Congress was regarded as a resounding success, far superior to the six preceding ones, and many felt that subsequent ones did not come anywhere near matching it. As President and the overseer of the Congress much credit for its success was attributed to Sir James Paget.

At the beginning of 1881 he was elected an Honorary Fellow of the Academy of Surgery of Philadelphia (January 3) and on 10 February he was made a Governor of St. Bartholomew's Hospital and it brought back memories of when he first came to the Hospital nearly fifty years previously. How his circumstances had changed. He was pleased to retire from the General Medical Council in June. It had involved a great deal of work but he felt that not much had been achieved. One of the items which was discussed was the introduction of the Conjoint Examinations and this seems to have influenced the students in rejecting him when he was put up as a candidate for the Lord Rectorship of Aberdeen University in October. It was felt that he was a supporter of the Conjoint examination which the students did not support.

He was appointed to the Hospitals' Commission in November; on the eleventh of that month he was elected an Honorary Fellow of the Medical Society of London and on 11 December was appointed an Honorary Member of the Reale Accademia di Medicina di Roma.

In November 1881 he suffered bronchopneumonia with haemoptysis and went to Nice in early December to recover. He and his wife stayed until early January and it was the first time they had spent Christmas away from their children. As usual, he spent much of his time writing long letters to his children and others describing the magnificent scenery. On his return to England his health had more or less returned to normal and he resumed his consultations and other responsibilities with his usual enthusiasm.

The number of honours bestowed on him increased throughout 1882. Among those were the honorary degree of Doctor of Medicine of the University of Wursburg. He was made an honorary Member of the Royal Society of Sciences of Upsala, of the Massachusetts Medical Society, of the Académie Royale de Médecine de Belgique, of the Aberdeen Medico-Chirurgical Society and of the Physiological Society.

On the 13 June 1882 he presented to the Medico-Chirurgical Society of London details of seven more patients with osteitis deformans. He attended the fiftieth anniversary meeting of the British Medical Association in Worcester in August 1882. The organisation had been founded as the Provincial Medical and Surgical Association in the boardroom of the Worcester Infirmary by Charles Hastings on 19 July 1832. In 1853 London doctors were allowed to join so, in 1853, it changed its name to the British Medical Association. Paget had attended many meetings of the Association over the years and was present at the meeting in Worcester in 1849 when Sir Charles Hastings was President.

In 1882 at the Jubilee Dinner he proposed the health of the British Medical Association in which he spoke about all that the Association had done for the Medical Profession over the years and the importance of the profession being self governing. He said "None can know so well as ourselves our need; none can know so well the remedy we require." His opinion was very interesting as he had served on the General Medical Council from 1876 until only two months previously and he was aware that the Council had been established to set and maintain standards required by all registered doctors. Paget made no secret of his dislike of the way the General Medical Council worked and no doubt his speech to the BMA was warning doctors that failure to regulate themselves might result in the GMC taking on this function. He said "It tells of feebleness, of cowardice, and want of self-reliance when we want to go to any Parliament living to help us."

At this stage in his life he was taking regular holidays and this summer he went to Crayford in Kent. Then in September 1882 he went to the south of France for two weeks with his brother, George. Three weeks later returning by train from Liverpool, where he had been to see a patient, he contrasts "Runcorn, grey almost to blackness, all mud below, all smoke above, lines of low red houses and huge chimneys, railways at every curve, heaps of refuse where lawns and trees should be" with the beauty of Avignon or of Canterbury where he had been two weeks previously.

In November he was on the panel to appoint the newly established Professor to the Department of Pathology in Cambridge and on 13 December he gave the first Bradshawe Lecture at the College of Surgeons to an audience of nearly five hundred. The title was 'On some Rare and New Diseases'. He felt that new diseases were found either because they had not been recognised in the past or that they were becoming more frequent and therefore more obvious. The increased frequency could be due, like Darwin's Natural Selection of Species, to inherent changes being passed on to future generations. Examples he gave of new diseases were Charcot's disease, osteitis deformans and gouty phlebitis. He refers to the work of Darwin and his prolonged period of observation of plants and animals throughout he world. Paget's successes had also resulted from critical observation throughout his life.

Although many of Paget's friends were politicians he did not like politics. At a meeting of the Metropolitan Counties branch of the British Medical Association on 17 January 1883 there was discussion of Sir George Humphry's proposals for the Collective Investigation of Diseases. Paget contrasted the practices of politicians with medical and scientific men who were not afraid to express their ignorance about a subject yet politicians would use such phrases as 'perhaps', 'possibly', 'I rather think', or 'I would venture to suggest'. They tried to cover up their ignorance. He went on to say that he felt that medical men were overlooking much valuable information by not recording information as they went through their lives. They had the opportunity of seeing many aspects of life but the significance of much of it was lost if it was not written down. He decries those who say 'I have no opportunity for scientific enquiry; I cannot investigate this; I can contribute nothing to that which I see the scientific members of the profession are doing.' Again, he refers to Darwin's work " It requires merely the opportunity of a practice in the country, and the mind and resolution of Darwin, to bring great pathological conclusions out of the most ordinary facts of daily life in general practice."

In April 1883 he was unanimously elected Vice-Chancellor of the University of London. It was a position of which he was immensely proud and he enjoyed it as it brought him into contact with many important and influential men. One of these was Sir Edward Fry who was impressed by Sir James's gentleness, courtesy and kindness in all matters and he appeared to dislike upsetting people. Sometimes this would result in him allowing discussions in committees to be prolonged. However he always had an open mind and might take some time to come to a conclusion but, when he did, people were reassured that he had taken all arguments into account. Nevertheless his belief in God was evident in all his actions and directed much of his life. He was a great believer in competitive examinations and Paget had benefitted from them as a student.

Dr. Pye-Smith said that although Sir James had been appointed a member of the Senate of London University in 1860, he seemed reluctant to express his views in his early years. However, he was influential on the Committee of the Faculty of Medicine in bringing in changes for the regulation of study and examination and in introducing the degrees of Bachelor and Master of Surgery. As Vice Chancellor Dr. Pye-Smith said "he soon made his influence felt. Punctual and constant in his attendance, cautious and deliberate in his statements, remarkable for his courtesy and tact, he yet showed a clearness of vision and quiet perseverance in the path he thought best chosen which made him as good a Chairman as could be." Dr. Pye-Smith also felt that Sir James's gentleness and dislike of upsetting people sometimes led to prolonged debate. Similarly, Sir Joshua Fitch said "his modesty and patience led him sometimes to be a little too tolerant of irrelevant speech, and to listen with scrupulous deference to the opinions of others, especially younger men who had given special attention to subjects and plans which lay outside his own range of experience." He went on to say he was "a prudent counsellor, and a gracious and conciliatory Chairman, one who cared much for the interests of the profession of which he was so distinguished an ornament, but who cared still more for the wider interests of learning and science, and for the consecration of all knowledge to high and noble uses."

In 1883 his summer holiday was in Leatherhead, Surrey after which he and Lydia went to Cornwall and Devon. That year the whole family was saddened by the death of the family nurse who had served them for so many years and was still living at Harewood Place at the time of her death.

The International Health Exhibition was held in 1884 and he was appointed a Vice President of it. He gave an address on 18 June in the Albert Hall at a reception given by the Prince of Wales for the International Juries of the Exhibition. The address looked at the relationship between the health of the nation and the work it did as well as the amount of work lost through sickness and early death. Obtaining the figures for this was extremely difficult and he used many sources. He estimated that 20 million weeks were lost annually as a result of illness but he found it impossible to accurately estimate how much this amounted to in monetary terms. He mentioned the death of children and said that as the country had more people than it needed some would say that the loss of children was not a problem. He decried this argument for, not only did it bring sorrow to the individual families, the doctor's duty was to promote health and save lives.

He concluded by discussing the various factors which had improved the nation's health in the preceding thirty years: better, cheaper and more varied food, less alcoholism, more clothing and an increase in recreation. Housing and drains were better, the water supply was cleaner as was the air. The work of the medical officers of health was resulting in great improvement as was the better treatment and nursing in hospitals and private homes.

On 17 April 1884, at the Tercentenary Festival of Edinburgh University, he received the degree of LL.D. In August he attended the Eighth International Medical Congress in Copenhagen where he addressed the Inaugural Meeting, proposed 'Denmark' at the President's Banquet and spoke at the great banquet given by the Municipality.

On his way to Copenhagen he visited Hanover and was impressed by its fine public buildings, wide streets and the beauty and quaintness of the old part of the town. However, Hildesheim was even better with its old houses and cathedral. He was equally impressed by beauty of the port of Hamburg which seemed to be far busier than any of the docks in London. After leaving Copenhagen he visited Germany and Russia. He went by way of Lubeck and Berlin to St. Petersburg where he marvelled at the great churches and museums with their collections of wonderful paintings. He thought Moscow outdid St. Petersburgh in the splendour and size of its churches and in the collections of the paintings. In contrast, the streets were dirty and drab and the majority of the citizens were poorly dressed. Leaving Moscow he went through Kiew to Warsaw and then to Dresden. This was a journey of great contrasts; the wealth in the churches and palaces in Russia against the abject poverty of many of its citizens.

Further honours came in 1885. On 19 June he was elected an Honorary Fellow of the Academy of Medicine in Ireland and on 23 March he was elected a Corresponding Member of the Académie des Sciences which he regarded as the highest distinction of its kind. He was elected an Honorary Member of the Deutsche Gesellschaft fur Chirurgie and on 6 August the Council of the College of Surgeons decided that a bust should be made of him. This was sculptured by Sir Edgar Boehm and for years it stood on the staircase of the College.

Bust of Sir James Paget by Sir Edgar Boehm
(Royal College of Surgeons)

This year also marked the new edition of the Pathological Catalogue which was made necessary by the addition of 1,750 specimens to the Museum. The work had taken another seven years and was done with the cooperation of Dr. Goodhart, Alban Doran - Pathological Assistant - and Mr. Eve who was Pathological Curator. They would meet on a Saturday afternoon, and sometimes on another day as well, when one of the three would read out the description of the specimen while Paget held it looking at it intensively. He insisted that the description should be complete and that nothing should be added. In addition he volunteered to do all the headings, references, cross-references and the index so he ended up doing most of the work.

11

REMINISCING

He was still a popular choice to give speeches and on 8 February 1885 he was asked to present the prizes to the Army Medical School at Netley Hospital. There he spoke of the importance of competitive examinations. Not only were there the formal examinations but, throughout his life, he was aware that he was being examined when having consultations with his seniors and that what he said and did could influence his opportunity for promotion. Similarly he was being examined in what he did in private practice and more particularly in the hospital when doctors and students would observe what he said and did and make assessments. At St. Bartholomew's Hospital he had instituted a system whereby on a certain day each week all patients requiring an important operation were brought to the theatre to be examined by the surgical staff who would then explain to the students what they felt was wrong with the patient and what should be the treatment. This was a great test of the surgeon's diagnostic ability, his therapeutic decisions and his presentation skills. Furthermore the students would be able to assess the outcome of the adopted procedure.

He went on to say that he was still being examined but now the majority of his examiners were young students and he was envious of the knowledge that they had and which he could not hope to attain. Knowledge was constantly changing and many opinions held twenty years ago were no longer found to be true. He took some comfort from the saying that 'even the youngest among us is not infallible'. He noted that while working abroad they would have the opportunity of picking up many facts and that it would be beneficial for the medical personnel in the army and navy services to mix with members of the medical profession, when they were back in their home country, as all three could learn much from each other.

He spent time reminiscing during a talk he gave to the Abernethian Society at St. Bartholomew's on 8 June 1885 when the title of his talk was 'St. Bartholomew's Hospital and School fifty years ago'. He referred to the nurses who fifty years ago were untrained and rather coarse. The sisters were somewhat better and did their best to help the patients and the young doctors. Improvements only came about as the result of the work and example of Florence Nightingale who brought in 'highly cultivated, courageous, and benevolent gentlewomen.' The medical students of his day were divided into three groups: those from Oxford and Cambridge University who were destined for the highest medical offices; the hospital apprentices who would become surgeons and the general body of students of which he was one. This last group were similar in behaviour and performance to those who studied law or went into business. Some behaved badly and were dismissed from the school, while others were idle and could not learn. The majority worked well and were probably little different from the present day students.

He felt that fifty years previously there was more drinking among the students and this was probably because there were so few other activities such as the provision of a boat or cricket club and the pursuit of athletics. The present day students had much more help and guidance in their training with better access to music and theatre but he doubted whether this resulted in them working harder than their predecessors. He concluded by saying "that those who have done best who have had the most single mind for the proper duties of their lives, and who, in striving after fitness for them, have cared least for the circumstances in which they were placed; who have used every help, but depended on none; and have set no limit to their work but the limit of their power". This would be a very apt description of James Paget as a student about how he applied himself to his studies and the success he achieved as a result.

His holiday that year (1885) was spent in Austria and Germany.

He finished writing his memoirs in 1886. These he had written in the evenings over a period of four to five years and three to four years later he gave them to one of his sons saying "Do what you like with them". He was elected an Honorary Fellow of the Royal College of Surgeons in Ireland on 8 March and on 29 June 1886 a Foreign Associate of the Académie de Médicine.

Having completed his memoirs and the new edition of the College Catalogue he started writing his 'Studies of Old Case-Books' which were based on private practice notes. He had kept meticulous notes which, in his early years, were lengthy and detailed and written on separate sheets of paper. Later, as his practice became busier, he wrote shorter notes often with abbreviations in big square note-books. He was very precise and neat in all that he wrote and everything was indexed. Every evening he would deal with his cases and write his letters before attending to any other writing or reading. In his later years he would dictate his letters in a very low voice, often in a whisper, while conversations and music would continue in the room. He would dictate to his surgical assistants and after he gave up operating in 1878 his secretary was his nephew, Dr. C.E. Paget. Later, his son Stephen would take on this duty. One of his surgical assistants between 1865 and 1870 was Mr. Marsh who said that it was not unusual to be writing 20 to 30 letters with him from 11.30 p.m. until 1.30 to 2 a.m. and then be expected to meet him at 7.30 a.m. or 8 a.m. to assist him operate in Brixton or Islington. The 'Studies of Old Case-Books' were completed and published in 1891.

In April 1886 Paget was appointed Chairman of the Pasteur Committee to assess Pasteur's work in treating rabies. Louis Pasteur (1822-1895) was a French chemist and microbiologist who had performed badly as a student but went on to show that infections were caused by micro-organisms. He then discovered the principles of vaccination, microbial fermentation and pasteurization and is regarded as the father of microbiology. He developed vaccines against chicken cholera and anthrax by using weakened forms of the bacteria which protected the chickens and the cattle respectively against the diseases. At this time a person bitten by a dog infected with rabies invariably died and he and his colleague, Emile Roux, developed a vaccine by injecting the virus into rabbits then weakening it by drying its nervous tissue. Trials on eleven dogs showed that the vaccine was effective when a nine year old boy, Joseph Meister, was bitten by a rabid dog. This put Pasteur in a difficult position, as he was not a licensed doctor, but he decided to vaccinate the boy on 6 July 1885 and his life was saved.

Paget had met Pasteur on a number of occasions and had exchanged letters over the years. Paget's committee consisted a number of leading figures, including Lister. The Committee decided to send three of its number to view Pasteur's work in Paris. One of the party was Victor Horsley (1857-1916) who was a young surgeon and physiologist who was secretary of the Committee. He did not smoke nor drink alcohol and became President of the British Temperance Association. He carried out many neuro-physiological studies and became a pioneer in neurosurgery. The Committee reviewed Pasteur's work and carried out a number of experiments which confirmed the accuracy of it. They also recommended that all dogs coming into the country should be quarantined and any thought to have the disease should be muzzled and isolated. These measures resulted in Britain becoming essentially free of the rabies within three years.

Paget was invited to unveil a statue of John Hunter in the University Museum of Oxford on 29 May 1886. He read a letter that John Hunter had written to Jenner, the discoverer of vaccination for the prevention of Smallpox. Hunter had been a student at St. Mary's Hall, Oxford attempting to study classics but he gave up after two terms. Paget said that the consequences of this were plain to see as his literary ability was terrible.

His summer holidays were spent in St. Ives, Huntingdonshire, the Pyrenees and the south of France. He always benefitted from his holiday. Before this one he could walk just over a mile but in the Pyrenees he could manage 15-20 miles on the mountain roads climbing up to 3,000 feet. In a letter to his brother, George, at the end of September he said he was having a consultation with a patient in Hong Kong which was going to be conducted by telegraph.

In 1887 the Duke of Westminster, Sir Rutherford Alcock and Sir James Paget were appointed trustees of the Women's Jubilee Offering to suggest the best ways in which it could help the public. They suggested setting up an institution for promoting the education and maintenance of nurses for the sick poor in their own homes. The institute became associated with the ancient Royal and Religious Foundation of St. Katharine's and right up to shortly before his death Sir James was an active supporter of it and rarely missed a meeting of one of its committees or of its council.

This year he was also President of the Pathological Society of London and in his inaugural address he commented on how Pathology had advanced since he gave his first lecture in Pathology forty years previously. Then it was regarded as little more than morbid anatomy yet "now there is work in it not only for the anatomist and physiologist, but the clinical observer, the experimentalist, the minutest microscopist, the statistician, the chemist, the naturalist, the historian, the psychologist and yet more."

In June he went to Ireland to receive the honorary degree of Doctor of Medicine of Trinity College, Dublin. He holidayed in Wimbledon, Lucerne, Innsbruck, Verona and San Martino.

In October 1887 he gave a talk at Owens College, Manchester about the importance of science. He stressed the importance to the students of using all their senses in accurate observation. This could only be achieved by continued practice and requires "careful self-training, self suspicion, and self-discipline". He went on to mention that he had been studying his old note books recently and he found he had made errors in observation and interpretation. For example, he had described typhoid ulcers of the intestines which were then considered to be associated with typhoid fever yet Sir William Jenner had noted that they were associated with another completely different fever.

He also decried those who said that a scientist could not be a business man, punctual, a plain speaker or anything else. "If a man of science cannot be business-like, it is the fault of his brain, not of his study; he would have been the same in any other pursuit in life." He then turned to his old message that the performance of a student dictates how a man will perform in practice in later life. "I have spoken of the methods of scientific study, of its machinery; but it may be asked, what is to be the force? What the driving power? It must be each man's will, by whatever motive stirred; when the will is wanting, the most perfect scheme is useless; and let me take a privilege of age, and say to the much younger who are here as students that this will must be used and cultivated now, and from first to last, and that the will is even much more important at first than at the last; for at last will becomes habit, as certainly for mental as it does for muscular uses. Such as the student is, such will be the practitioner." He supported this by the study he had carried out on 1,000 of his previous students which showed that for the majority of students their performance then reflected their success or lack of it in the future. From the poor results that Louis Pasteur had as a student he would have been an exception to the rule.

On 3 March 1888 he gave the annual address to the London University Extension students speaking about science and the wonderful powers of the brain which were little understood.

He returned to Yarmouth at Easter and stayed at the Victoria Hotel on the seafront. In a letter to one of his sons on April 6 he said how much they were enjoying themselves with wonderful weather. There was also the customary east and north-east wind. He had taken a long walk through the town and was disappointed to find that many fine houses had been extended into shops and that "a busy and important place of commerce and shipbuilding is a fishing-place and sea-side watering-place." He went into the old family house on the quay and found that the only old decorations remaining were "a beautiful Italian marble chimney-piece, and the drawers and closets of the great store-room."

Over the years he received many invitations to visit America and in 1888 he nearly did but he feared the journey would be too much for his wife and he would not want to go without her. This was the last year they had their usual long holiday in Europe which consisted of long walks and sight-seeing. They went to San Martino calling in at Schaffhausen, Berne, Grindelwald and Botzen on the way. However, he did not give up his Continental visits completely for he went to Paris in 1889 for the Exhibition; he attended the Tenth International Medical Congress in Berlin in 1890 and in 1891 he went all the way to Rome for a consultation with a patient.

On 20 September 1888 he opened the new, larger hospital in Yarmouth which replaced the one opened in 1840. It had been built on the mount which was part of the fortifications built just outside the old town wall at the end of the sixteenth century in response to the threat of invasion by the Spanish. He probably saw the building of the original hospital on one of his visits to the town and certainly visited it. In spite of being extended, this hospital was too small for the town's needs and a decision was made to replace it with a much larger one to celebrate Queen Victoria's Jubilee. The foundation stone was laid by the Prince of Wales on 18 May 1887 and to help raise funds for the hospital the public was able to buy tickets for reserved seats at five shillings each. Unreserved seats were available at half price.

Sir James Paget was the obvious choice to open the new hospital. He was born in Yarmouth, grew up there and did his apprenticeship for nearly five years to a local doctor and surgeon. Now he was one of the leading surgeons in the country and, in his honour, one of the wards was named after him. Before the opening, a service was held at 11.30 a.m. in St. Nicholas Church where the Dean of Norwich preached. His text was from the Psalms; 'he healeth the broken in heart and bindeth up their wounds'. Paget was presented with a silver gilt key to open the front door of the hospital at 12.30 p.m. After this, at 1.30pm, there was a luncheon for 300 people in the town hall at which Paget made a speech in which he said "Yarmouth fifty years ago, was one of the first places in the land for medical teaching and that the present medical men had a reputation to maintain." In the afternoon, between 3 and 5 p.m., the public was allowed to visit the hospital which had 42 beds.

**Yarmouth General Hospital on opening day
20 September 1888.**

The new hospital was extended several times over the years and eventually had 135 beds and was known as the Great Yarmouth General Hospital. In the 1960s and 1970s it dealt with General Surgery, Ears, Nose and Throat Surgery, Gynaecology, Paediatrics and had the Accident and Emergency Department. Medical patients, and later the obstetric patients, were cared for at Northgate Hospital which had originally been the workhouse. In the 1970s Great Yarmouth General Hospital and nine small hospitals scattered around the district provided the hospital care for a population of just over 200,000. This was thought not to be practical and, after a visit by Dr. David Owen, the Health Minister, the new District General Hospital was built at Gorleston-on-Sea - half way between Lowestoft and Great Yarmouth. The new hospital received its first patients on 21 December 1981 and on 3 September 1984 the District Health Authority agreed to name it the James Paget Hospital. The District General Hospital opened by Paget was eventually sold for £250,000 and pulled down in 1984. On the site were built flats for elderly people.

In May 1889 he was appointed to the Royal Commission on Vaccination under the chairmanship of Lord Herschell. Its purpose was to decide whether vaccination was safe and effective and whether it should be compulsory for everyone. Vaccination for smallpox had resulted from the work of Dr. Edward Jenner (1749-1823) who noted that milkmaids who had contracted cowpox had a mild disease with skin lesions similar to smallpox which seemed to protect them from developing smallpox. In 1796 he decided to follow John Hunter's advice "Don't think; try" by carrying out an experiment on eight year old James Phipps, his gardener's son. He took fluid from a cowpox pustule and placed it on an incision on the boy's arm. Two month's later Jenner injected James with smallpox and he did not develop the disease. Jenner repeated the experiment in other people and eventually it became widely adopted. Inoculation against smallpox had been introduced into Britain by Lady Mary Wortley Montagu in 1721 who had noticed the practice of variolation in Istanbul where her husband was British Ambassador. This involved transferring a small quantity of fluid from a smallpox pustule to a healthy individual. Some people developed an immunity to smallpox but others died. In 1840 variolation was banned in favour of vaccination.

The Royal Commission on Vaccination continued its work until the Final Report was published in August 1896 and the last of the Appendices was completed in 1897. To enable him to do this work he resigned from the Council of the Royal College of Surgeons where he had sat for 24 years. There were 136 meetings of the Royal Commission and he chaired 39 of the last 40. Initially Paget was in favour of vaccination being compulsory for everyone but soon came round to, and supported, Lord Herschell's proposal for a 'Conscience Clause' - allowing people to opt out of vaccination - which proved to be effective. In 1979 the World Health Organisation declared that Smallpox as a disease had been eradicated.

Paget's dedication to any appointment he took on and the manner of his working is covered by Jonathan Hutchinson, one of his students who was later a surgeon at the London Hospital. He served with him on the Commission and said this about him "he never accepted an appointment without zealously attending to its duties. He was regular and punctual on all occasions, and no one whom I have ever known could express views more clearly or tersely, or make more sure of their effect. Many a discussion which threatened to be interminable was concluded by a few chosen words from his lips. He did not speak often, and never lengthily, nor did he ever take up much of the time of the Commission in cross-questioning the witnesses. He was always a most attentive listener, and if ever a question of his own was interposed, it went to the heart of the matter."

Very similar views about him were expressed in the Times obituary on 1 January 1900 in referring to his work on the College Council. "Paget's management of other men and of affairs was very skillful, and depended to a great extent upon his constant willingness to listen to argument and to reconsider his options. No one could yield to adverse pressure with a better grace, and he never seemed to be so possessed by an idea as not to be able to throw it aside. Perhaps he was rather too fond of compromise, and he has been known to express wonder how men could so easily persuade themselves that their own views must of necessity be correct. In the Council of the College of Surgeons he exercised great influence, which was partly due to his inclination to be with the majority. He went with the tide to a considerable extent, and would seldom persevere in an opposition which seemed unlikely to be successful; not from the slightest inclination towards time-serving, but from genuine intellectual modesty, which led him to distrust his own judgement, and to think of the probability that others might understand the question at issue better than he did himself........ In questions of right, however, he admitted of no compromise: and, both by precept and by example, he invariably upheld the highest standard of professional honour and integrity."

To celebrate Louis Pasteur's treatment for rabies a meeting was held at the Mansion House on 1 July 1889 at which Paget spoke. Pasteur wrote to thank him for his contribution. This was one of many letters that he wrote to Paget over the years and they were always written in French. This was one of the many advantages he had of being conversant in several European languages. It enabled him to read and understand foreign scientific papers from his student days and allowed him to actively participate in debates at many of the international meetings he attended. This gave him an advantage over many of his British colleagues.

He was elected an Honorary Member of the Medical Society of Constantinople on 29 July 1889 and within two weeks he was holidaying in Lowestoft, a fishing and holiday town ten miles south of Yarmouth. He walked 8-10 miles daily and visited many haunts of his youth such Burgh Castle, where there is a well preserved Roman fort, the beautiful Oulton Broad and Corton, a village on the coast just north of Lowestoft. Burgh Castle was one of the places where he had collected plants as a teenager in his survey of plants in and around Yarmouth which he published in 1834.

He attended the International Medical Congress in Berlin during August 1890 and in letters to his wife he frequently said how much he was missing her. He met up with many of his friends, such as Lord Lister and Prof Virchow, and complained of the overwhelming heat of one session which was held in a circus-like building lighted by electricity and gas with no windows and only one entrance in which there were 5,000 delegates.

In September he holidayed at Robin Hood's Bay, Yorkshire and had the company of his grandsons to whom he introduced the delights of observing nature. While there he saw his friend Mr. Cooper, who was Sir Astley Cooper's grand-nephew. The following month he gave an address at University College, Liverpool emphasising the importance that science should not be separated from medical practice. Again he stressed the importance of "careful observation and cautious thinking." He decries the fact that some people speak as though they had never overlooked anything of importance and suggests that it would be useful to have a book containing "not a history of discoveries, but a history of oversights".

He wrote a short appreciation of Pasteur's life and work in Nature in March 1891 and within a few weeks Pasteur had written to him in French saying that he had it translated and thanked him for it. He said how honoured he felt that Paget should write such an article.

He went to see a patient in Rome in April. It was a long and tiring journey and he regretted that he could not share the beauties of the city with members of his family.

This year he was Chairman of the Virchow Testimonial Fund to celebrate Virchow's seventieth birthday. Rudolph Carl Virchow (1821-1902) was a German pathologist, statesman and one of the most prominent physicians of his time. He was a leader of social and political reform and showed the importance of good public health for which he strongly campaigned. Paget had been his good friend and colleague for many years and wrote an article on 'Scientific Study in the Practice of Medicine and Surgery' for the three volumes of the Festschrift in Professor Virchow's honour.

For his summer holiday he went to Sidestrand near Cromer which is on the North Norfolk coast. From here he wrote to one of his sons who was unable to join the family party saying how important it was to have a 'complete holiday' although he adds that it is always necessary to include some meaningful study time.

Some years before, he had started writing essays based on his old case notes. This was not an easy task and at least one of his assistants had failed to 'make something' of them. Eventually 'Studies of Old Case-books' was published in 1891. His aims in writing this book were to draw attention to certain diseases and injuries which might not be well known and to suggest 'probable lines of enquiry, or of some general principles' to the younger members of the profession. He also hoped that the essays might stimulate some of his contemporaries to 'do similar but better work with their old case-books'.

Many topics were covered including periostitis after strains, irregular pulse, Spines Suspected of Deformity, the Use of the Will for Health and Errors in the Chronometry of Life. He explained that lateral curvature of the spine was at least 20 times more common among young women than in young men, especially among the richer classes. He thought that this was due to the habit of ladies sitting upright with their backs unsupported whereas young men sat in various postures and participated in many athletic pursuits which strengthened their back muscles. He therefore recommended that the young ladies should be allowed to follow the pursuits of young men and he would advise the mothers "bring her up like a boy".

In the essay on how will could influence health and disease he refers to people who have an 'ear for music'. They often have an increased sensitivity to pain and this could be increased like the person who is trying to improve his appreciation of music. Eventually, improvement of both abilities could become involuntary and, if there is to be an improvement, it is necessary for the will to try to take control.

He visited Yarmouth again in August 1891 and stayed at the Victoria Hotel. He was saddened at how the town's social and commercial aspects had deteriorated. Hardly any of the great houses on South Quay were still private houses, there were no large ships and the ship-building yards seem to have gone. As far as the beach north of the jetty, where Nelson had landed, was concerned it appeared to be worse than Margate. However, he was impressed by St. Nicholas Church, which he thought was beautiful and conducted fine services. In addition, the town walls and old Tolhouse were much better preserved than they had been. He wrote to his brother, George, suggesting that both of them might visit the old town in October or November and they did that in October 1891. It would be the last time they visited the town together for Sir George became ill on 16 January 1892 and died on 29 January aged 83 years old.

James Paget always had a strong affection for George and wrote about him to Sir Henry Acland. "He was, indeed, admirable in all his life, and those most near to him might well think him faultless. He was, for many years, the main stay of the whole family; the only one who had power to help the rest. But for him, I doubt whether I could have studied my profession, and yet, in all the years that have since passed, I never heard a word or seen a look that would remind me of my deep obligation to him. His end was like his whole life - gentle, pious, watchful for the happiness of all around him - just such as one may wish to imitate with truth."

James went to Dublin in July 1892 representing London University at the Tercentenary Festival of Dublin University. He spoke for 'Great Britain, and her Colonies and Dependencies' at a presentation of addresses by Delegates representing 74 Universities and Academies. He had a holiday at his brother George's house in Wales before touring Hampshire and Cornwall with his eldest son, John.

He returned to Oxford in November 1892 to give the inaugural address at the newly formed Oxford Medical Society.

This was held in a large room of the University Museum on 11th November at 8.30 p.m. Sir Henry Acland (1815-1900), Regius Professor of Medicine, presided over the meeting and introduced his friend as the 'Nestor of British Surgery'. Acland was also a Fellow of the Royal Society, had sat with Paget on the Royal Commission on Sanitary Laws in England and Wales and had been President of the General Medical Council. He had also played a leading part in the revival of the Oxford Medical School. Paget started by saying how pleased he was to renew old friendships in Oxford and how grateful he was to Oxford for the happiness it had given to his sons in studying at the University. Paget's theme was the importance of science and practice working together. They were not incompatible and the increased instruction of basic sciences in the medical schools would help the integration. Regular meetings of doctors, as was one of the aims of the new Society, would also help.

In 1893 he returned to his brother's house in Wales for a further summer holiday. He also holidayed at a cottage in Hampstead owned by Sir J. Russell Reynolds.

Registration of Nurses was being debated this year and in a letter to Sir Henry Acland he said he could not understand why this should not be done as doctors had been required to be registered for some years. He was amazed that Florence Nightingale (1820-1910), with whom he had worked well over the years, was opposed to the registration of qualified nurses. Eventually she changed her mind. She and James Paget had exchanged letters regularly for over thirty years and were on very friendly terms.

She had returned from the Crimea in 1856 where she had witnessed the appalling sanitary conditions and frightful wounds which became infected and from which the majority of soldiers died. Her work there, with her team of nurses, improved conditions and reduced the mortality. On returning to England she set about improving nursing, raising standards of hygiene and the design of hospitals. She set up the Nightingale School of Nursing at St. Thomas' Hospital with public subscriptions. She was very keen to obtain hospital statistics and Sir James was the first to help her in this task. He arranged for a registrar to be appointed at St. Bartholomew's to provide and publish accurate statistics. Her admiration for Sir James is indicated in the inscription she wrote in her book on 'Lying-in Institutions' in 1871 in which she says: "To Sir James Paget whose Sanitary eminence in furthering the health and improving the Statistics of Hospitals is as great a subject for admiration as his Surgical eminence is to all Europe this little book on Lying-in Institutions with the earnest request & hope that he will spare a little of his invaluable time & mind to criticize it unsparingly is offered by the most devoted of his followers. Florence Nightingale London. Oct 10/71."

> To
> Sir James Paget
> whose Sanitary eminence in furthering
> the health & improving the statistics
> of Hospitals
> is as great a subject for admiration
> as his Surgical eminence
> is to all Europe
>
> this little book
> ON
> LYING-IN INSTITUTIONS.
> with the earnest request & hope
> that he will spare a little of his
> invaluable time & mind
> to criticize it unsparingly
>
> is offered by
> the most devoted of his followers
> Florence Nightingale
> London
> Oct 10/71

Florence Nightingale's handwritten dedication to Sir James in her book 'Lying-In Institutions'

12

OLD AGE

By 1893 both he and his wife were beginning to feel the consequences of their increasing age and Harewood House was really too big for them. Several years before he thought the ideal place to move to would be a house near the British Museum but, in September, he and his wife moved to 5 Park Square West, Regent's Park. This was a much smaller house with a conservatory and he continued to see some patients there. It also enabled Lydia to continue seeing her friends.

In April 1894 he visited Yarmouth for several days at the time of the Easter Fair. He went again in August and then on to Wales. This year marked the last address he gave to students and it is fitting that it was to the Abernethian Society. It was sixty years since he had first spoken at the Society when he was in his first year as a medical student and presented his paper on Trichina spiralis. In 1894 he spoke on one of his favourite themes that science and practice should not be divorced from each other. He said "It is often said or implied that, in our profession, a man cannot be both practical and scientific; science and practice seem to some people to be incompatible. Each man, they say, must devote himself to the one or the other. The like of this has long been said, and it is sheer nonsense."

His wife, Lydia, died peacefully on 7 January 1895. They had been married for just over fifty years and it was a very happy marriage as is indicated in this letter Lydia wrote to her children in October 1880. "Forty-four years since we were engaged! and forty-four years it seems, I must own, with its crowd of untold blessings, the times of sore trial, the poverty, the riches (comparatively), the times of weariness, the elation of feeling rested, the onward progress of our most dear children, the many loved ones gone, the far greater number spared to our exceeding joy, the many changes that have marked our lives. And what a strange thing, in this imperfect state of being, to be able to speak of one's having more gentle love, more confidence, more sweet dependence on one, than ever. The long years have not worn all these great sources of joy out, but the stream of even, mutual love seems uninterrupted. May God so grant us peace to the end, and then order all things mercifully for us, that our end may be according to His will, 'free from sin and shame and, if it be His pleasure, free from pain', or such pain as shall disturb or distress those around us." Here she shows that she shares the same philosophy as her husband that she does not want to be a burden to others.

Lady Paget
(Wellcome Library, London)

In his memoirs he wrote of her "In May 1844, I married, and began to enjoy that happiness of domestic life which has already lasted without a break, without a cloud, for 39 years. From this time, the "being alone" was the being alone with one who never failed in love, in wise counsel, in prudence and in gentle care of me. With her it was easy to work and be undisturbed by anything going-on around me; a habit I can advise everyone to learn . . . She wrote for me, copying for the press my roughly written manuscripts, sitting with me till midnight or far into the morning."

He returned to Yarmouth in April 1895 and this was to be the last visit to the town of his birth. He wrote "To me, each day brings strange states of mind, in the contrasts of all I see and hear with the memory of the same things from 60 and 70 years ago. Nothing is just what it was; and it is not possible to keep one's thoughts exclusively on those which have changed for the better. The sea-shore is much further off; the Roads (These are areas off shore where the larger ships used to anchor and where they received some protection from the rough North Sea by the sandbanks further out to sea such as Scroby Sands) have fewer ships in them; some of the best views are hidden by new buildings: most of the best old houses are turned into shops: - but these and other deteriorations are, or may be, outweighed by many signs of improvement, and the unfailing beauty of some of the scenery, such as that about the harbour and the rivers and marsh-lands and Breydon (The large estuary draining the rivers Waveney, Yare and the Bure) and the old Burgh Castle, and some others, which we have been able to see in charming weather. And all the deteriorations are only consistent with my own, as the signs of old age accumulate and increase in me - my slow small writing, my slow and sometimes shuffling walking, my shorter breath, and many more, which, while I study them, I try to use as good lessons: may God help me thus to use them alright." In his writings he was noting the deterioration in his health and perhaps wondering how much longer he would live.

Throughout the 1890s his health slowly deteriorated and reading an account of these years is reminiscent of Shakespeare's 'Seven Ages of Man'. Physically he was getting weaker, his eyesight was deteriorating, he was finding it increasingly difficult to write yet his mind was still active. For as long as he could he would dress every morning, in case a patient came to see him. He also had visitors and would like to go in his carriage around London and into the country.

In the summer of 1895 he holidayed in Bude and in Wales. In October Louis Pasteur died. Each had thought a great deal of each other and he was keen to go to the funeral but, because of the deterioration of his own health he thought it unwise to make the long journey to Paris, and did not go. This year St. Bartholomew's Hospital named a ward after him and when he attended the centenary meeting of the Abernethian Society on 1 May he received a great welcome from the students.

In 1896 his younger daughter and his grandson, Michael Thompson, were living with him at Park Square West and they and his other children enabled him to stay in his home, along with the help of Nurse Finn who joined the household in March 1898, until the day he died. His awareness of and his preparation for his impending death were illustrated in the letter he wrote to Sir Henry Acland in September 1896. "I am, thank God, well, and may have been refreshed, in some measure, by my holiday. But I am growing very old, and, as I watch the changes that old age brings, I constantly feel sure that they are such as one should be thankful for - including as they do the consciousness that the 'time draweth near', and that, in the short time that may remain, there is very little claim or need for the work that almost wholly occupied one's earlier days, and that one's mind is wholly unfit for the study of such subjects as used to be one's delight and seemed to be one's duty, and that thus and by various other means one is being taught how best to use the time thus mercifully granted and, as it were, divinely set apart and exactly fitted for its best use. I believe that we are agreeing in this thought and in many that issue from it."

The Royal College of Surgeons of England awarded him the Honorary Gold Medal of the College in April 1897. This was the highest honour that they could award and was much prized by him. This was the last year he had a holiday when he went to stay in Wales. In March 1898 he resigned from the Board of the Clerical, Medical and General Life Assurance Society of which he had been a director for 34 years and Deputy Chairman for 6 years. However, he remained a Life-Governor of Epsom College, President of the British Medical Benevolent Fund and President of the Society for the Relief of Widows and Orphans of Medical Men.

Until the beginning of 1898 he would insist on getting properly dressed in the mornings and dressing for dinner in the evening. He would keep himself busy with writing and reading and seeing the occasional patient. However from March of that year it was becoming increasingly difficult to keep up these appearances. His voice had become a whisper and he had difficulty in walking unaided yet he would make light of his infirmities and would often joke about them. Most evenings there would be some music in the house and people would come in and talk with him. By this time he had a white beard and would sit in his dressing-gown with a rug over his knees. Beside him would be some books, his watch, some flowers and his glass of wine. Most of his reading at this time would be from the New Testament and his books of devotion. The image is similar to that which he had written about his father in his Memoirs. "In the time of his natural decay, nothing erred from its just proportion in the work of life; only there gradually became less of everything belonging to this life; and in due time everything slowly and coincidentally ceased."

Most days he would like to be taken in his carriage on tours around the city, especially to see his old hospital, St. Bartholomew's, or into the country to visit Kew, Richmond or Dulwich. He preferred these drives if a friend or visitor could go with him. In May 1898 the Prince and Princes of Wales went to visit him and in April 1899 he met up with many of his old friends, including Lord Lister, Sir William Priestley, Sir Samuel Wilks, Sir Henry Thompson and Sir Hermann Weber among others.

During the autumn of 1899 he became weaker. He had difficulty in eating and lost the use of his right hand. However, on Christmas Day he was driven to the house of one of his sons where two of his grandchildren spoke a prologue in his honour. The next day he had a slight fever and signs of congestion. From this time he stayed in bed and received communion from his son, Francis the future Bishop of Oxford, shortly before he lost consciousness on 29 December. He died peacefully on the evening of Saturday, 30 December 1899. His estate was valued at almost £75,000.

His funeral was held in Westminster Abbey on 4 January

1900. It was conducted by his son Francis and attended by many of his old colleagues and the leading members of London society. His fame and influence also reached to the young, for medical students from St. Thomas' Hospital came across Westminster Bridge and stood bare headed as his coffin was transferred to Finchley Cemetery where he was buried beside his wife.

EPILOGUE

James Paget was born into one of the wealthy families of Great Yarmouth but by the age of ten his father was having financial difficulties and he began to understand what poverty meant. However, he went on to become one of the leading surgeons in the country and his contributions to pathology were recognised world wide. What were the reasons for his success? What are his legacies?

REASONS FOR SUCCESS

His success can be attributed to his genes, his home and early life, his religious faith and, above all to hard work. Each had varying influences on him but all were positive.

Genetic Influences

From his father he inherited the ability of clear thinking and a belief in himself which enabled Samuel Paget to become a successful business man. His mother had a flair for art and this ability to draw and paint was passed on to James - enabling him to illustrate his lectures - and to several of her other children. The two outstanding children in the family were George and James. The former became a well known physician and Regius Professor of Physic in Cambridge. His grandson, Sir George Paget Thomson FRS (1892-1975) was a highly distinguished physicist and received the Nobel Prize in 1937 for proving the wavelike properties of electrons. However, it could be argued that George Thomson's success was inherited from his father, Sir Joseph John Thomson, OM, FRS (1856-1940), who was also awarded the Nobel prize for Physics in 1906 for the discovery of the electron and his work on the conduction of electricity in gases.

As far as James is concerned, all his six children were successful in different ways. John, his eldest son, was a successful barrister and writer; Francis became Bishop of Oxford; Henry Luke became Bishop of Stepney and then of

Chester and Stephen became a surgeon but is better known as a writer. The second daughter, Mary, was musical and was involved in charity work. The Bishop of Oxford had two sons. Sir Bernard Charles Tolver Paget, GCB, DSO, MC (1887-1961) was a general in the army and Commander-in-Chief of Middle East Command from 1944 until 1946. His older brother, Edward Francis (1886-1971) was appointed Bishop of Southern Rhodesia in 1925 and in 1955 was elected the inaugural Archbishop of Central Africa.

Home and early life

James had the good fortune to be part of a happy family living in a large house beside a flourishing seaport which was a base for the Royal Navy and had a thriving fishing industry. He had the opportunity of mixing with men of high intelligence, such as Dawson Turner; artists of the calibre of John Crome and his son John Berney Crome; naval officers and the family doctor, Charles Costerton. He also saw the poor side of Great Yarmouth, where many people lived in poverty in the rows which stretched east west across the town. The houses were often inhabited by several families, there was little or no sanitation, the insides were dark - as the rows were very narrow - and death and disease were common. However, wealth did not protect the family from illness and early death. Samuel and Sarah had seventeen children yet eight died soon after birth or by the age of four. Arthur died of consumption aged 25, Charles died aged 33 years - having suffered from osteomyelitis of his femur for many years - and Francis, a sufferer of epilepsy died suddenly after a short illness. Thus in his early years James was able to witness at close hand many different aspects of life.

In spite of the death of many of his sibs, life in the large house on the quay from all accounts seemed to be a very happy one. The children played well together and were encouraged to study and read. Most of them had lessons in drawing and painting but perhaps the most important lessons James received were seeing how his mother arranged and catalogued her many possessions. She had a vast collection of autographs, seals, shells, corals and agates, old china and glass and curiosities of all kinds. Years later James recounted how they were orderly arranged and labelled.

An even greater influence on his later life was the study he undertook with his brother Charles on the animals and plants in and around Great Yarmouth. It introduced him "into the society of studious and observant men; it gave me an ambition for success..... it encouraged the habit of observing, of really looking at things and learning the value of exact descriptions; it educated me in habits of orderly arrangement........My early associations with scientific men; my readiness to work patiently in museums, and arrange them, and make catalogues; the unfelt power of observing and of recording fact; these and many more helps towards happiness and success may justly be ascribed to the pursuit of botany." He said that the knowledge of knowing the names of the plants and their appearance "was useless: the discipline of acquiring it was beyond price."

Religious faith

At the start of the nineteenth century religion played a large part in the life of most families. The Paget family regularly attended services at St. Nicholas Church, which is situated at the north end of the market place. It could seat 4,000 people yet was not large enough for the town so in 1714 St. George's Chapel was built. It is likely that there were regular bible readings in the home and family prayers. It is probable that James' deep faith started and developed here and throughout his life he was a practicing Christian and studied theology. His son, Francis, the Bishop of Oxford, said of him "No trait in the tenor of my father's life was more constant and characteristic than his use of Sunday. So far as he rightly could, he kept the day from the encroachment of ordinary work. He did what had to be done: but he never lightened the burden of a week-day by deferring any of its demands till Sunday. There was a peculiar look of reluctance in the way he went to see a visitor who had come on that day when he might as well have come another: and the visit was generally short. I remember asking him when I was an undergraduate whether I might on Sunday go on reading for the Schools: I do not remember the answer: but it was decisively negative; partly on the ground that a man was almost sure to break down if he would not rest one day in the week. And he used religiously the rest he so secured. He never dined out, never travelled for pleasure's sake, never read a newspaper or a novel on Sunday, never let any weariness stop his Church-going........

"And with his habitual study of theology went, in a like tendency, two deeper habits, of which it would not be well to say much: the habit of reverence, and the habit of devotion. As the thought of what he was in these ways rises in one's mind, it brings the picture of a grace and beauty of which one longs to speak: but even a little knowledge of what he felt about it makes one sure that it is better to be silent: and the words seem coarse and blundering when they touch it.... But all his strictness and carefulness in these ways was but the partial expression of a trait that was wrought into his heart and mind: a trait that gave a quiet and natural sanctity to all his thinking about great things. Only those who were nearest to him could even guess at the intensity and simplicity of that inner life."

Hard work

From an early age he seems to have been able to concentrate and study while others might be playing. No doubt his mother had an influence here because he said of her "the qualities which one best remembers were her intense love of her children, her marvellous activity and industry, her admiration of all that was beautiful in art and nature, her skill in writing, needlework and painting." So at home he witnessed the great 'activity and industry' of his mother.

At school he was not very impressed with his teacher, Mr. Bowles. The education "was not of a very high order; neither was it accurate or profound or of a kind likely to encourage deeper study." Nevertheless, when it was thought that he might have a career in the Royal Navy he read books which covered science and navigation. During his apprenticeship he taught himself French so well that he was able to translate Bichat's General Anatomy into excellent English and the notebook, written in his beautiful writing, is preserved at the Royal

College of Surgeons. In addition, he began a study of the plants and animals in and around Great Yarmouth with his brother Charles. This work brought him into contact with Dawson Turner, Sir William Hooker and other famous men and it made him realise the benefits of hard work which, undoubtably, was a stimulus to studying even harder.

His various note books and papers in the Royal College of Surgeons of England show how neatly he wrote. Rarely is there a crossing out or correction and this continues with all his writings throughout his life. It indicates a well-trained mind which is not distracted and is able to concentrate on the matter at hand. During his second year of apprenticeship he attended lectures on bones by the young surgeon Randall in the Angel Inn, Great Yarmouth. His very detailed notes are written in the same neat hand used in writing letters throughout his life. They start with Lecture 1 on 22 January 1833, with the second on 25 January and continue through to the fourteenth lecture on 4 March.

When he went to St. Bartholomew's he was not particularly impressed by most of the lectures so spent much of the time learning from books. He said that during his time as a student there were not many distractions to studying and if there were he did not have the money to make use of them. Therefore, he spent the time studying and won almost all the prizes in his first and second years. Here again he realized the benefits of studying hard.

Throughout his life he repeatedly said how much joy he had in working and this is immortalized in this motto 'Work itself is a Pleasure'. Many times he referred to idle and lazy students and few could have worked as hard as he did. He had the great ability of doing things at the time rather than later. For example, each evening he would write up the notes of the patients he had seen that day and write letters to their doctors. This was never a duty to be deferred. In later life he found this increasingly difficult and in a letter written on 1 December 1896, at the age of nearly 83, he wrote "I ought to have written to you yesterday, but I am becoming an example of what I used to observe in others - how little men do except under compulsion, or something that they feel equivalent to it. I have now almost nothing to do, and I leave the 'almost' undone, even at the cost of good manners."

He was also extremely tidy and this is illustrated by the fact that he did all of his work on the dining room table taking up no more than two and half feet. Apart from a break at 10 p.m. to read prayers he would continue writing his notes and letters until they were all done and would then read and do some further writing until one or two o'clock in the morning.

It was not until 1868 that the family took a holiday together and then holidays became a regular event. Nevertheless, it was expected that everyone would spend the morning reading and writing and this was often repeated in the evenings.

Thus, hard work was instilled in James from a young age. He saw the benefits and what could be achieved by it and really enjoyed doing it. Moreover, he seems to have been successful in instilling these virtues in his children.

LEGACIES and ATTRIBUTES

The legacies of Sir James are found in science, medicine, education, his family and several other places and will be discussed separately.

Science

Sir James is regarded as the father of British Pathology. He developed his great powers of observation at home, stimulated by his mother's energy to collect and classify her many possessions, and this ability was further advanced by the work he did on the flora and fauna of Great Yarmouth in his teens. This led to the publication of his book with his brother Charles in 1834. In many ways it is fortunate that his father was in financial difficulty otherwise he would have been able to pay for James to become a house surgeon which would have speeded his way into becoming a surgeon. He would then not have benefitted from the many years he spent in the dissecting room and in the museums of St. Bartholomew's and the Royal College of Surgeons. These years of study enabled him to learn anatomy in great detail and to observe the changes brought on by disease. Not only did he observe but he questioned his findings such as when he noted the speckles of calcification in the diaphragm of a man who had died of tuberculosis. These had been noted for many years but no one had actually looked closely and questioned what they were. He did this with his hand lens and as St. Bartholomew's did not possess a microscope he traced one down at the British Museum. This is also an example at how quickly he worked as he first observed the worm with his hand lens on the 2 February and four days later he was reporting his results to the Abernethian Society at the hospital on the 6 February 1835.

As a child he had noticed how his mother had arranged and recorded all her possessions. He was, therefore, well prepared to carry out cataloguing all the specimens in the museum at St. Bartholomew's. Years later he referred to his ability of observing and orderly arrangement at which he became so skilled. Later, he was asked to do the same for the College of Surgeons museum which had at its core the specimens collected by John Hunter. The work of cataloguing all the specimens in these two museums was immense but brought him great knowledge and understanding. This was extended by the lectures he gave to the students at St. Bartholmew's. Initially these were given in the dissecting room and were based on the specimens he had dissected earlier in the day.

He was one of the first to make wide use of the microscope so he was able to see changes in tissues and organs which had not been appreciated before. This enabled great advances to be made into the understanding of the pathological processes and here he was in the vanguard.

Another advantage that Paget had over most of his colleagues was a good understanding of languages. He was able to read and converse in French, German and Italian so was able to keep up to date with advances in Europe. He exchanged letters with most of the leading scientists of the day and later on met them at many of the scientific meetings he attended.

He brought together many of his discoveries and what was known about pathology in the series of lectures as the Arris and Gale Professor of the College of Surgeons, a position he was elected to over six successive years. The lectures were published each year and he brought them together at the end in two volumes entitled 'Lectures on Surgical Pathology' on 1853. This became the standard work on Pathology and greatly enhanced his reputation as the leading pathologist of his day.

However, Paget was not only a pathologist. He became an authority on Physiology as well. This had started when he was writing for the Medical Review where he would be reporting on recent advances in physiology. This continued with his appointment as a lecturer in Physiology which required him to read all the latest books and papers on the subject. He was always questioning what was said and written and devised experiments to check their validity, many of which he did with the students. His lectures formed the basis of Kirkes' Handbook of Physiology which became the leading work on the subject. Thus, through this book and his 'Lectures in Surgical Pathology', both of which went into many editions, he was influencing the education of many medical students for years to come.

Education

When he arrived at St. Bartholomew's as a medical student in 1834 the medical school was not doing well. Most of the consultants were not interested in teaching and many students attended the private schools for their tuition. By 1843 the situation had deteriorated further and few students entered for the anatomy lectures. One of his fiancée's brothers suggested the establishment of the collegiate system as in Oxford and Cambridge. The governing body agreed to this and on 8 August 1843 he was appointed the first warden. He was the guide and mentor to the students. Most responded well and those in the college did academically far better than those who were not. By his time he had become a popular and an accomplished lecturer. Not only did he have the knowledge of the subjects he taught but he had a wonderful way of delivering what he had to say. In addition he would illustrate his lectures with drawings, demonstrations on pathological specimens and experiments on tissues and animals.

Added to this he was interested in the welfare of his students and this brought out the best in them and an affection for him. He also supported them in their careers after they had qualified. He would greet them with a warm smile and often a hand shake.

He was an excellent and popular lecturer and teacher and his lectures were always well attended. Not only did he teach knowledge he seems to have inspired many students, many of whom kept in touch with him over the years. It seems likely that many of his methods and practices were passed onto future generations.

He was the first person to review the success or failure of over a thousand previous students by following them up many years after they had left the medical school. He kept records of what he thought of each student and then compared this with how well they did in later life. His conclusion was that in most cases the behaviour of the person as a student dictated how they would do in later life. What was important was the will of the person to succeed. He put it this way."In remembering those with whom I was year after year associated, and whom it was my duty to study, nothing appears more certain than that the personal character, the very nature, the will, of each student had far greater force in determining his career than any helps or hindrances whatever. All my recollections would lead me to tell that every student may draw from his daily life a very likely forecast of his own life in practice, for it will depend on himself a hundredfold more than on circumstances. The time and the place, the work to be done, and its responsibilities, will change; but the man will be the same, except in so far as he may change himself."

Paget also had a big influence on postgraduate education. When he was appointed examiner for the East Indian Company he and his co-examiners were appalled at the knowledge of the young surgeons. He set down various standards and the way in which they were to be assessed. This, initially, caused an uproar in the colleges and medical schools as it indicated that they were not teaching and examining the young surgeons properly. It also meant that there were insufficient suitably qualified surgeons to run the medical services for the East Indian Company. Eventually Paget and his colleagues won the argument and other bodies followed the examples they had set.

Thus he had a large influence on postgraduate training and assessment. He was also an advocate of the conjoint examination to be run by the Royal Colleges of Surgeons and Physicians as an exit an examination from medical school for young doctors. This gave students an alternative means of qualifying as a doctor.

Practice of Medicine

Paget was able to bring his vast knowledge of pathology and physiology into his practice of medicine and, coupled with his great powers of observation, he became one of the most highly regarded clinicians of his day. His opinions were sought from doctors and patients throughout the country and often in Europe. Repeatedly in his speeches, lectures and writings he stressed the importance of combining science with practice. They should not be kept separate and the knowledge and application of science makes for a better doctor.

With the attributes he had gained from his outstanding knowledge of pathology, which had enabled him to understand the processes of diseases, and his knowledge of physiology, which helped him to understand how the body worked, coupled with his great powers of observation, he was able to bring together the symptoms that the patient described with what he found on examining the patient. These are the two essentials in arriving at a diagnosis. He was one of the first to employ this tactic and it was even more important in his day when there were very few investigations available. Today, the clinician has access to CT and MRI scanners and many exotic blood tests but the best clinicians are those who first talk with the patient, observing all the time, and thoroughly examine them before reaching for the investigation request form. Such a process can save time and money in the long run. Paget's methods of reaching a diagnosis are as valid today as they were 150 years ago.

He was also insistent upon absolute honesty and, in a lecture to students on calamities in surgery, he criticized his colleagues who tried to cover up their failings. Referring to those surgeons who said "I did my best; but these things will happen" he remarked that "there is no more miserable or false plea than this...but there are some people who seem to have a happy art of forgetting all their failures, and remembering nothing but their success, and, as I have watched such men in professional life, years have always made them worse instead of better surgeons. They seem to have the faculty of reckoning all failures as little, and all successes as big; they make their brains like sieves, and they run all the little things through, and retain all the big ones which they suppose to be their successes; and a mischievous heap of rubbish it is that they retain."

He was always a very courteous man and, although he was rather business like in his consultations at home, he showed care and compassion for his patients. He was particularly concerned for the care his patients received and emphasized the need to treat them gently, particularly in changing dressings or moving a patient with a broken limb. He was one of the first in Britain to use Plaster of Paris for the immobilization of a limb with a fractured bone. He was very particular about cleanliness on the wards, for which he held the house surgeon responsible, and showed by his practice and example how to look after patients.

He believed in looking at the whole patient, which is now looked upon as the holistic approach, and in an address he gave to the Abernethian Society in 1885 he said "As no two persons are exactly alike in health so neither are any two alike in disease; and no diagnosis is complete or exact which does not include an estimate of the personal character, or the constitution of a patient. There used to be a French saying that 'French physicians treat the disease, English the patient.' So far as this is true it is to the honour of the English, for to treat a sick man rightly requires the diagnosis not only of the disease but of all the manner and degrees in which its supposed essential characters are modified by his personal qualities, by the mingled inheritances wrought in him by the conditions of his past life, and by many things besides."

He also believed in the presence of a higher authority in determining health and, in the seventh lecture of his Lectures on Surgical Pathology, he speaks of his religious convictions. "Let me suggest that the instances of recovery from disease and injury seem to be only examples of a law yet larger than that within the terms of which they may be comprised; a law wider than the grasp of science; the law that expresses our Creator's will for the recovery of all lost perfection. To this strain of thought we are guided by the remembrance that the healing of the body, was ever chosen as the fittest emblem in His work."

Many hundreds of students and young doctors would have observed this and been influenced by his practice.

In his early days of practice patients were looked after by untrained women. Florence Nightingale (1820-1910), after returning from the Crimea, started training ladies to take up nursing with dramatic improvements in standards of patient care. Paget was a strong supporter of her efforts and felt that there should be an organisation to oversee the training and registration of nurses long before Florence Nightingale came round to these views. He wrote on pressure sores describing the type of patient that was more likely to develop them and how to prevent them. He even suggested the development of a water bed to try to prevent pressure sores. Here again he was ahead of his time.

He was a great believer in the therapeutic value of wine and especially of port wine. He recommended it to his father in his later years and to his brother George when he was ill. He took his own advice and felt the benefit of a daily port after dinner.

Surgery

His son, Stephen, said "he was a surgeon and a man of science, and one cannot imagine him wishing to be anything different." He was always emphasising the importance of combining science with practice. However, he had the disadvantage of having had little training in surgery. During his medical student days he was not impressed by the teaching of the surgeons and spent most of his time on the medical wards or reading his books. He did not have the money to become an apprentice or a house surgeon and his first real opportunity to do any proper surgery was when he was appointed an assistant surgeon. However, in the years leading up to that time, he had spent most of his time in the dissecting rooms, the museums, teaching the medical students and reading. Therefore, he had an extremely sound knowledge of anatomy which would have helped his surgery, and his understanding of pathology and physiology helped him in making diagnoses and managing his patients. Another advantage of the delay in starting surgery was that by this time - 1847 - ether and then chloroform had been introduced as anaesthetics so that patients could undergo surgery without pain and agony previously experienced. It also meant that the surgery did not have to be rushed, dissection could be much more refined and a wider range of operations could be undertaken. His surgical legacy is that he stressed the importance of introducing science into medical and surgical practice which helped in obtaining more accurate diagnoses and better management of the patient.

Description of diseases not made before

Paget is best known for his descriptions of osteitis deformans and changes in the nipple associated with breast cancer. However he described eight other conditions which had not been appreciated before. Most of these discoveries resulted from his great powers of observation, his meticulous record keeping and the fact that he saw so many patients that his chances of seeing a previously unrecognised condition was increased.
Trichina spiralis. For years people doing postmortem examinations had been aware of speckles of calcification in muscle. James, as a first year medical student, wondered what was the cause, and looking with his hand lens and later a borrowed microscope, noted the cysts containing the tiny worm. He dissected the worm from the cyst and made drawings of his findings. Years later in his Memoirs he said "All the men in the dissecting-rooms, teachers included, 'saw' the little specks in the muscles: but I believe that I alone 'looked-at' them and 'observed them': no one trained in natural history could have failed to do so."
The evening of his discovery he wrote about it to his brother, George, and four days later he presented his findings to St. Bartholomew's Abernethian Society. Unbeknown to him

Tommy Wormald, the senior demonstrator, took samples of the muscle to Richard Owen, lecturer in comparative anatomy, who also noted the worm and presented his findings to the Zoological Society and named the worm Trichina spiralis. Twenty-five years later Virchow and von Zenker completed their work on the life cycle of the worm showing how humans became infected with it by eating contaminated meat, especially pork, and that it could be prevented by cooking the meat properly. Thus the observations of a first year medical student started the search for how a worm infected humans and how it could be prevented.

Paget's Disease of Nipple. Over many years he had noted in a number of women a "rawness of the areola of the breast" which was followed within two years by the development of a breast cancer. He reported "about fifteen cases" in 1874 in the St. Bartholomew's Hospital Reports and thought that the cancer was stimulated by the chronic irritation around the nipple. In this he was wrong as it is now known that it is extensive carcinoma in situ predisposes to the cancer and that invasion of the epidermis of nipple by these cells causes the ulceration. What is surprising is that in this paper there is no reference to microscopy of the nipple lesions as Paget was always promoting the use of the microscope to aid diagnosis and help in the understanding of disease. The results of the microscopy of these lesions was given two years later by Henry Butlin one of his previous house surgeons.

Only 1-2% of breast carcinomas are associated with eczematous-like changes in the nipple but recognition of this appearance enables investigations - such as biopsy, mammography ultrasound and MRI scans - to be done so that the cancer can be detected in its earliest stages and treatment carried out. As the disease is often multifocal, mastectomy is usually the treatment of choice.

Extramammary Paget's Disease. In his 1874 paper on the association between the rawness of the areola of the breast and breast cancer he refers to a "persistent rawness of the glans penis, like a long-enduring balanitis, followed after more than a year's duration by a cancer of the substance of the glans". In 1889 Radcliffe Crocker described a patient with a similar lesion involving both the the penis and scrotum which was seen by Paget. It is an extremely rare condition and Weiner, writing in the American Journal of Cancer in 1937, was able to find only three other reported cases of Paget's disease of the male genitalia.

Similar appearances are seen in the anogenital areas, particularly the vulva, and in the axillae. The condition presents like eczema with intense itching and is associated with thickened plaques that become red and crusty. All of these areas contain apocrine glands and the breast is a modified apocrine gland. The appearance under the microscope of these lesions in the anogenital area and axillae is similar to that found in the nipple with large Pagetoid cells. However, the exact origin of the neoplastic cells in extramammary Paget's disease is still debatable. It is thought that they may arise from intraepidermal parts of sweat glands or from primitive basal cells. The main treatment is wide local excision, although radiotherapy is sometimes used. Although Paget's name is associated with these extramammary lesions in the anogenital areas and in the axilla there appears to be no record that he noted them.

Osteitis Deformans. Paget presented five cases of Osteitis Deformans in a paper to the Medico-Chirurgical Society in 1876 and he reported a further seven in 1882 to the same Society. In the first paper he describes a man he had followed for twenty years since 1854. In the two papers he covers all the main features of the disease, except for fractures, but in the first paper there was an unusually high incidence of malignancy (Three of five patients). He describes the patients having aches and pains in the limbs, some of which become enlarged and bowed. In the patient followed for twenty years the skull became enlarged, the patient began to stoop and developed a large mass in the left forearm which at postmortem was confirmed to be a malignant tumour which had spread to the chest and skull. In this paper he describes the microscopy findings and he thinks the changes are due to an inflammatory process. Unlike osteoporosis - which is a progressive bone disease causing a decrease in bone mass and density - which affects the whole skeleton, osteitis deformans affects only some bones. It is caused by an excessive breakdown and formation of bone with disorganized remodelling.

At present there is no cure for Paget's Disease of Bone but many of the symptoms can be relieved by drugs, such as biphosphonates and calcitonin. The cause of the disease is still unknown but viruses have been suggested and there appears to be an inherited tendency.

Paget was the first to draw attention to a disease that affects between 1.5% and 8% of populations. Since then it has been found in the bones of Egyptians who died several thousand years ago. It has also been suggested that a lady, whose portrait by Quinter Massys (1465-1530) is in the National Gallery, London, may have had Paget's Disease of the skull. Again his powers of observation and record keeping allowed him to present a number of patients with similar symptoms and so describe a new disease.

Osteitis Dessicans is a condition in which part of the articular surface of a joint - most commonly the knee - becomes separated and lies loosely in the joint causing pain and sometimes 'locking' of the joint. In 1558 Ambroise Paré removed loose bodies from a knee joint but it was first described in 1738 by Alexander Monro (primus) (1697-1767) in 1738. He was the founder of the Edinburgh Medical School. Paget reported on two children who had loose bodies in their knee joints in 1870. The girl used to break pieces of wood over her knee. The boy was athletic with "many blows and strains to his knee from sports." Paget asked "How can such pieces of articular cartilage be detached from living bone? They cannot be chipped off - no force can do this. These bodies are sequestra exfoliated after necrosis of injured portions of cartilage without inflammation." He described it as 'quiet necrosis'. Later, in 1887 Franz Konig (1832-1910) published a paper on the causes of loose bodies in the joint describing it as a subchondral inflammatory process and naming the condition osteitis dessicans. Subsequently, the condition has been described in many other joints and, although trauma is felt to be associated with it sometimes, it is thought that interruption of the blood supply to parts of the cartilage may be the underlying cause. Although Paget was not the first to describe loose bodies in joints he appears to have been the first to discuss the possible causes for them.

Apophysitis of the Tibial Tubercle was first described by Paget in 1891as a painful condition at the insertion of the patellar ligament to the upper end of the tibia. It occurs mainly between the ages of nine and sixteen years of age and is more prevalent in boys. It results from repeated avulsion fractures of the tubercle which makes it extremely tender. The symptoms usually resolve over two years.

It is now known as Osgood-Schlatter disease after Robert Bayley Osgood (1873-1956), an American orthopaedic surgeon, and Carl Schlatter (1864-1934), a Swiss Surgeon, both of whom described the condition independently in 1903. However, Paget described the condition twelve years previously and his original description in his 'Studies of Old Case-Books', published in 1891, covers most of the features of the condition. The first chapter deals with Periostitis Following Strains and, after dealing with some examples which in several instances sound like tuberculous abscesses rather than periostitis, he goes on to write "Cases such as these, proving so grave injury of periosteum and bone after strains, may be enough to make it sure that strains of less severity, or in healthier persons, may produce many degrees of less, yet not unimportant, damage. An excellent example was in an elderly gentleman who came with a well-marked circumscribed periosteal swelling - a node it might have been called - on the inner border of his tibia, which had formed quickly after a severe night cramp in the muscles of the calf. Much more common are the enlargements of the tubercle of the tibia which are often seen in young people much given to athletic games. They complain of aching pain at and about the part, especially during and after active exercise, and the tubercle may be felt enlarged and is often too warm. The pain often continues for many months, and there may be enlargement of the bursa under the ligamentum patellae, and the tubercle may remain too prominent; but common as are these cases, especially in our public schools, I have never known grave mischief ensue in any of them, and they get well of themselves. They may represent one of the least degrees of periostitis due to strain; the increase of the prominence of the bone is only just beyond that which may be deemed the normal limit for the attachment of vigorous muscles."

Later on he discusses whether sporting activities should be controlled as these strains seem to be provoked by athletic activity. As usual, he has a very sensible view on the matter which should be directed to the present day health and safety lobby and the leaders of schools. "So many of the injuries of which I have spoken occur in athletic sports, that I may be expected to write urgent protests, and even claims to some sort of legislation. I am not disposed to do anything of the kind. The advantages, both moral and muscular, of the free and self-managed games in our schools are immeasurably greater than the disadvantages of the occasional damages done in them. And the pleasures of nearly all sports and the associated ambition for success in them are augmented by a consciousness of some danger. In schools, ordinary prudence on the part of masters playing with the boys, or looking on may suffice; especially if they are careful about those who are evidently weakly in their health. After school-life, men must be trusted for self-care in sports."

Carpal Tunnel Syndrome results from compression of the Median nerve as it passes through a tunnel created by the bones of the wrist behind and the transverse carpal ligament in front. The compression results from narrowing of the tunnel by e.g. damage to the bones by arthritis or fracture, or by increase in size of the tissues within the tunnel e.g. obesity, diabetes, ganglia and hypothyroidism. Pressure on the nerve results in pins and needles, numbness and pain in the thumb, index finger, middle finger and half of the ring finger. As it becomes more progressive there is wasting and weakness of some of the muscles of the thumb. Patients frequently wake with the pins and needles in their hands which can be relieved by shaking their hands.

Paget was the first to recognize that the median nerve could be compressed at the wrist. He described this in his Lectures in Surgical Pathology Vol.1 London: Longmans, Brown, Green & Longmans (1853). "In the College Museum (No. 2177) is the hand of a man, whose case is related by Mr. Swann, the donor of the preparation. The median nerve, where it passes under the annular ligament, is enlarged, with adhesion to all the adjacent tissues, and induration of both it and them. A cord had been drawn very tight round this man's wrist seven years before the amputation of the arm. At this time, it is probable, the median and other nerves suffered injury; for he had constant pain in the hand after the accident, impairment of touch, contraction of the fingers, and (which bears most on the present question) constantly repeated ulcerations at the back of the hand.

"Mr. Hilton told me this case: A man was at Guy's Hospital, who, in consequence of a fracture at the lower end of the radius, repaired by an excessive quantity of new bone, suffered compression of the median nerve. He had ulceration of the thumb, and fore and middle fingers, which resisted various treatment, and was cured only by so binding the wrist that, the parts on the palmar aspect being relaxed, the pressure on the nerve was removed. So long as this was done, the ulcers became and remained well; but as soon as the man was allowed to use his hand, the pressure on the nerves was renewed, and the ulceration of the parts supplied by them returned."

Putnam, in 1880, described 37 patients with nocturnal or early morning numbness of the thumb, index and lateral part of the middle finger along with other characteristics of median nerve compression but it was not until 1933 that Learmonth reported an operation to divide the transverse carpal ligament which was causing the compression, so relieving the patient of their symptoms.

In the second patient that Paget describes he notices that the excess bone formation which developed following the fracture of the lower end of the radius bone caused the pressure on the median nerve and so the symptoms and signs which were noted. It is not known whether these facts were learnt during a postmortem examination or whether the man's arm was removed because of his symptoms as appears to have been the case with the first patient. Fortunately today, the condition can be treated by splinting, injection of local steroids or by division of the transverse carpal ligament under local anaesthetic.

Paget-Schroetter Disease is a condition where there is thrombosis of the deep veins of the arms, usually the axillary and subclavian veins. It usually occurs in fit young people and more often in males. Paget first described it in a 27 year old soldier in 1858 who made a complete recovery. He repeats the description in a paper on 'Gouty and some other forms of phlebitis' in 1866 in the St. Bartholomew's Hospital Reports volume 2 page 82 and again in his Clinical Lectures and Essays in 1875. Von Schroetter suggested that the syndrome was due to occlusive thrombosis of the subclavian and axillary veins. In recent years the incidence of the condition has increased due to the insertion of catheters into the subclavian vein to deliver intravenous nutrition and chemotherapy. It can also be brought on by repetitive movements and by compression between the first rib, the clavicle and the serratus anterior muscle. Treatment is usually by long term anticoagulants.

Paget Recurrent Fibroid Tumours. Paget describes a number of tumours which appear to be halfway between obviously benign and maligant tumours in his lectures on Surgical Pathology first published in 1853. He likens them to the spindle-celled sarcomata of Virchow. The first patient had a tumour close to the tibia which was removed when he was 60 years old. It recurred five times and eventually he requested that his leg be removed but he died a few days later. The second patient was a man of 28 who had a tumour removed from his shoulder. Three local recurrences were removed. When it recurred again it was decided to leave it. Many years later he was well and the tumour had not increased in size.

A third man had a tumour over the anterior aspect of the right first rib which was removed in 1839. It recurred four times and subsequently appeared fixed to the clavicle with a discharging wound and he died in 1852. Another man of 45 years of age presented in 1843 with a tumour over his scapula after a fall. It was removed as were four recurrences. A sixth tumour appeared and the patient died in 1850.

A 22 year old lady presented with a tumour over the left lumbar region which she had had for three years. It was removed in 1832. Two subsequent recurrences were removed and a similar tumour removed from the right breast in 1868. In 1870 (According to the third edition of the book) when the lady was in her sixtieth year she had no evidence of the tumours.

Some of these patients were described by his colleagues and

he gives other examples. In all the microscopic appearance is of elongated spindle shaped cells.

Paget Residual Abscesses. Paget writes about residual abscesses in his book 'Clinical Lectures and Essays' in which he says "Under the name 'residual abscesses' I would include all abscesses formed in or about the residues of former inflammations." He describes abscesses affecting the lumbar spine which result in marked kyphosis and psoas abscesses both of which were almost certainly tuberculous in origin. Similarly, chronic discharge from cervical lymph nodes is probably tuberculous. Other residual abscesses he mentions are from bones and here he is describing chronic osteomyelitis.

Diseases on which he had influence

Rabies. Paget was appointed chairman of the Pasteur Committee in 1886 to assess Pasteur's work on Rabies and to make recommendations. The committee sent a three man delegation to Paris to review Pasteur's work. The committee recommended the use of Pasteur's vaccine for cases of rabies, that all dogs coming into the country should be quarantined and that any dog suspected of having the disease should be muzzled and isolated. As a result of these measures Britain became essentially free of rabies within three years and Paget, as chairman of the committee, can take a large share of the credit for this.

Vaccination for Smallpox. In May 1889 Paget was appointed to the Royal Commission on Vaccination to assess its value and to decide how best to devise a programme for it. The Commission sat until 1896 and he chaired 39 of the last 40 meetings so had a big influence on the outcomes. Initially he thought that vaccination should be compulsory but came round to the view that people could opt out if they had particularly strong views. So successful was the programme that the World Health Organisation declared in 1979 that smallpox as a disease had been eradicated.

Vivisection

As a physiologist, Paget had carried out experiments on living animals and, as the study of physiology became increasingly popular, the number of experiments on animals increased as did the opposition from the Anti-vivisectionists. This reached its height in 1875 when Paget was President of the Royal College of Surgeons. As a prominent surgeon and the leader of his profession what he said and did mattered. The same year a Royal Commission on Vivisection was set up and Paget spoke in favour of there being some form of legislation to control vivisection. The Bill in its initial form would have handicapped the work of scientists but modifications were made to it after Paget, Joseph Hooker and Burdon-Smith had a meeting with the Home Secretary. Their action was to have a profound beneficial effect on science for years to come.

In further efforts to counter the activities of the anti-vivisectionists the Association for the Advancement of Medicine by Research was established in 1882 with Paget as the Vice President and some years later his son, Stephen became its secretary.

His Children

James and Lydia Paget had four sons and two daughters. They were all brought up on a strong work ethic and either through this, or their genes, or perhaps a combination of the two, they all became successful people. Even on holidays they were expected to spend the morning reading and studying and many evenings they had to do the same. Their father had strict religious principles which influenced the running of his house and it is interesting that his eldest was married to a vicar and two of his sons entered the church and ended up as bishops.

Catherine Paget was their first child and she was born in 1846. In 1877, at the age of 31, she married the Reverend Henry Thompson who had been a school master and became the vicar of St. Mary the Virgin, in Oxford. It is the largest parish church in the city and the University Church. They had three sons:

James (1878-1956), Henry (1880-1958) and Michael (1881-1951).

John Rahere Paget was born on 9 March 1848. His second name indicates the St. Bartholomew's connection as the monk Rahere was the founder of the hospital. In 1872 he completed an Arts and Law Degree at Cambridge before going to the Inner Temple. He became a barrister and author and wrote 'The Law of Banking' in 1904 which is still regarded as the leading publication on banking law. The thirteenth edition was published in 2007. He married Julia Moke in 1883 and they had three sons and two daughters. John Rahere became the second baronet in 1899 on the death of Sir James and his eldest son, James Francis (1890-1972), became the third baronet on John's death in 1938. Sir James Francis Paget was a captain the Royal Navy and married in 1943 Frances Alexandra Hamilton Fraser (1890-1972). She was the widow of Frederick David Stewart Sandiman (1908-1932) who had died at the age of 23 years in 1932. James Francis and Frances had no children so on his death in 1972 the baronetcy passed to his cousin, Julian, the grandson of Sir James' second son, Francis, who was the Bishop of Oxford. Sir Julian is the present and fourth baronet. He is an ex soldier and is the author of nine books. He and his wife, Diana, have two children, Olivia born in 1957 and Henry born in 1959.

John Rahere's elder daughter was Margaret (1889-1970) who married Kenneth Churchill and they had three children: John, George and Susan. His younger daughter was Winifred (1896-1986) who married Bernard Paget (Third son of Francis, the Bishop of Oxford). Their two sons were Julian Paget (4th baronet) and Tony who died in 1945 from wounds sustained at the end of the war. John Rahere also had two other sons: George (1890-1964) and Rupert (1891-1903).

Francis Paget was born on 20 March 1851 and educated at Shrewsbury School before studying at Christ Church, Oxford. He was an eminent scholar, Regius Professor of Pastoral Theology at Oxford University and Dean of Christ Church before becoming Bishop of Oxford in 1901. He married Helen Church and they had four sons and two daughters. His second son, Bernard Charles Tolver Paget (1887-1961), was a well known general. He fought in both World War I and II and ended up commanding the Middle East Command. He married his cousin Winifred (1896-1986), the fifth child of John Rahere, the second baronet. His son, Julian, became the fourth baronet in 1972, whose features closely resemble Sir James and perhaps this is due to receiving a double dose of Paget genes.

Sir Julian Paget unveiling bust of Sir James
(James Paget University Hospital)

The Bishop of Oxford's other sons were Richard (1884-1959), who married Jean Holden-Ross and then Eruder Saumier, and Humphrey (1891-1985) who married Elizabeth Dibden. His daughters were Beatrice (1885-1954) and Freda (1889-1910).

Henry Luke Paget was born on 18 October 1853 (St. Lukes Day) and this date made Sir James wonder whether his son would follow him and become a doctor. After schooling at Shrewsbury he joined his older brother at Christ Church, Oxford. He was ordained in 1877 and two years later went to the Leeds Clergy School as vice principal. In 1881 he was in charge of the Christ Church Mission for the poor in Poplar, living in East India Dock Road, before becoming vicar of St. Pancras in 1882. He used to give his Father communion at his home each week during his last years. He became Bishop of Stepney in 1909 until he became Bishop of Chester in 1919 at the age of 66years. He continued there until 1932 when he was 79. He died in 1937. He married Elma Hoare in 1892 and they had two sons, Samuel and Paul. Samuel was born in 1895 and died in 1918. Paul Edward Paget, was born in 1901 and rebuilt many of the churches in London that were damaged during World War II. He married Verily Anderson in 1971 and died in 1985.

Stephen Paget was born in July 1855 and followed his second and third brothers to Shrewsbury and Christ Church, Oxford where he read classics. He studied medicine at St. Bartholomew's where he became a house surgeon. For a time he was secretary to his father then became surgeon to the Metropolitan Hospital and to the West London Hospital. Later he gave up general surgery and became an ear surgeon at the Middlesex Hospital. He seems to have struggled to make a success as a surgeon in London as he was a very sensitive and cultured individual and resigned his hospital appointments. Like his father he had a very orderly mind, was a good speaker and an excellent writer. His classics training at Oxford no doubt helped in this. Above all he was a superb organiser and was the power behind establishing the Research Defence Society which held its first meeting at his home, 70 Harley Street, on 27

January 1908. This was really the successor to the Association for the Advancement of Medicine with which his father had been associated when the anti-vivisectionists were such a force. Much of his time over the next few years was spent organising and speaking at meetings for the Society and editing its journal 'The Fight against Disease'.

He was a prolific writer and specialised in biographies. In 'Memoirs and Letters of Sir James Paget', first published in 1901, he reproduces the memoirs written by his father and brings together many letters and articles written by and to him along with lengthy comments by Stephen. He wrote biographies of John Hunter (1897) Ambroise Paré (1897), Sir Victor Horsley (1919), Pasteur (1914) and his brother Francis, the Bishop of Oxford (1902). In 1905 he wrote the history of the Royal Medical and Chirurgical Society from 1805 to 1905 and Confession Medici (1908) is possibly a reflection on his own life.

In at least one field Stephen was ahead of his time. He studied the notes of 735 patients who had died of breast cancer and found that in the majority metastases developed in the liver rather than in other organs. From this he developed the 'soil and seed' hypothesis and wrote "When a plant goes to seed, its seeds are carried in all directions... But they can only live and grow if they fall on congenial ground." He published this work in the Lancet in 1889 at a time when it was believed that it was the malignant cells which stimulated the tissues and organs to become malignant. If that were the case, he argued, then metastases would be distributed equally throughout the body rather than in selected organs as he had demonstrated. In spite of this, his views were not accepted for many years. His work mirrors that of his father's whose observations and great knowledge of pathology enabled him to make ground-breaking discoveries.

During the 1914-18 war he lectured on hygiene and typhoid inoculation before running the Anglo-Russian Hospital in Petrograd during 1916 and 1917. Unfortunately, his health broke down again and he retired to Limpsfield in Surrey where he died in 1926 several years after having a stroke. He had married Eleanor Mary Burd in 1885 and they had two daughters: Eleanor (1888-1919) who married Bertie Howarth in 1909 and Dorothea (1890-1931) who married Basil Mayhew in 1911.

Mary Maud was their last child and she was born in May 1860. She was an accomplished musician, wrote articles on musical history and worked with charities. During the 1914-18 war she organised concerts in hospitals and camps and after the war this was continued in 'Music in Villages'. She did pioneering work in girls' clubs and became totally blind in middle age. She lived with, and looked after her parents, and died at the age of 84 in 1945.

Caring for others and Friendships

Throughout his life James showed great caring and compassion for his family, friends, patients and strangers. He showed love and respect for his parents and, along with his brother, George, spent many years paying off his father's debts. It was not uncommon for him to not charge some of his poorer patients and others were sometimes given a handful of coins. Each day he left home he would make sure he had some coins which he could give to beggars in the street.

James Paget was friends with Royalty, the top scientists and medical men of the age as well as prominent politicians and many literary people, artist and musicians. He associated with many of the top people in society, many of whom regarded him as a personal friend. No doubt the fact that his father-in law was chaplain to the Duke of York helped his introductions to the Royal Family and may have helped his early appointment as a surgeon to Queen Victoria but there was genuine friendship here, particularly with the Prince of Wales, who frequently attended his addresses and meetings and was a guest at his house.

Stephen Paget, his youngest son, said he was "for 41 years a member of the household of Her Majesty Queen Victoria, and for 36years a member of the household of H.R.H. the Prince of Wales: a very old and very dear servant and friend. He loved to be in his place at the Court, and to be welcome there both for his own sake and for his long record of services. In a letter to his brother, he defines his loyalty as wholly personal and non-political: but it was so far political, in the original meaning of the word, that it was in keeping with that spirit in him which has been described, in a very different context, as this spirit of order, this hearty acceptance of a place in a society, this proud submission which no more desires to rise above its place than it will consent to fall below it. Wherever he went, he liked to be taken as a surgeon: and if he had chosen any other profession, he would have upheld, with the same steady insistence, the dignity of work and of the professional life, as the thing that place a man."

Scientists became his friends as they frequently met at meetings and exchanged letters and Paget had an advantage over many of his colleagues as he was able to read papers and converse well in French, German and Italian. These colleagues also admired the ground-breaking work that he had done as a young man and continued to do as a surgeon. Especial friends were Pasteur, Virchow, Darwin, Huxley, Sir Joseph Hooker and Rokitansky. Among his closest literary friends were George Eliot, who sent him copies of her books, Lord Tennyson, who had been one of his patients and subsequently sent him copies of his poems, Ruskin, Browning and many others. As he became older and had more free time he started to read novels, both English and French, and other non-medical works, and seemed to enjoy them.

He had a poor view of many politicians and politics but Gladstone and Lord Palmerston were great friends of his. He had first met Gladstone in 1846 when the two were among a group founding the House of Charity in Soho, London. Gladstone was often a guest at his house and he attended his Hunterian Oration. After one of his several stays at Gladstone's house he wrote a letter on 1 September 1896 saying "The great pleasure of our holiday is not ended: every recollection of it brings happiness and gratitude. It is useless to try, and I will not try, to tell you how much I thank you for all your loving care of me; you gave me more happiness and rest than I could have thought now possible in this life. Our visit to Hawarden was certainly an event that we may all remember, and may sometimes make others happy by telling of." It is perhaps surprising that he was approached to stand for parliament on two occasions - once as a Conservative and once as a Liberal - but he declined. His brother, George, also turned down an offer to represent the University of Cambridge in Parliament in 1887.

Paget's involvement in medical politics was not one he would have chosen but, being on the council of a number of national bodies, it became a necessity. As in all things he worked hard to improve matters and his wise advice was eagerly sought. He was in favour of progress yet he disliked confrontation, but he felt he had played his part in improving teaching, examining and in the general management of the affairs of the College and the University of London. Nevertheless he felt the progress obtained was not commensurate with the time spent. He felt this particularly so with the General Medical Council.

His interest in art went back to his youth when local artists came to the house on the quay and gave lessons in drawing and painting. He, and many of his brothers and sisters, became accomplished artists themselves and Paget found that this ability was a great help in illustrating his lectures. As he started to holiday in Europe one of his passions was to visit old churches and art galleries and see the great works by the masters. In London he was frequently in the company of the leading artists of the day and George Richmond, Holman Hunt, Sir Edgar Boehm as well as many others he regarded as friends.

He was meeting medical people throughout most of his life. Many were just colleagues but he had particular affection for Sir William Gull, Sir Thomas Smith and Lord Lister. He had a close relationship with Florence Nightingale and supported her in improving the standards of nursing. He was a pall bearer for the funerals of Tennyson and Browning but was unable to do this for Darwin.

Over the years he was appointed or elected to various national bodies, such as the Councils of the College of Surgeons, the Royal Society, the Medico-Chirurgical Society as well as many others. All of these required many hours of his time although Paget remarks that many men appointed to these positions failed to carry out their duties responsibly.

Clearly this work load was a great strain on him and in later life he questioned whether he could have continued at such a pace. A severe infection caught during a hospital post mortem in 1871 made him ill for three months and was the trigger for him to decide to give up his hospital practice. Soon after his retirement he was made a baronet but he feared that people would think that this honour indicated that he had retired and his private practice would suffer. Consequently, he determined to work even harder on his practice and his earnings increased each subsequent year until he decided to give up operating seven years later. He did this as he was finding it increasingly difficult to keep up to date and, physically, he was finding the work more difficult. It was for similar reasons that he decided to give up his consulting work some years later.

Public Speaking

It is not possible to hear him speak but several people wrote about his great oratory and many of these talks and lectures were published and can be read. His son, Stephen, recalls the beauty of his public speaking, "the distinction and refinement, the exact choice of the right words. His voice was clear, and musical within a narrow range of notes; not very strong, not deep or resonant; but measured, quiet, and as it were always in time and in tune; and his slight Norfolk accent was part of the pleasantness of it. ....He had few gestures; only, he would sometimes raise his hand, or rest his chin on it, till some grave sentence was finished."

Another person wrote about his speech making. "His attitude and action were simple and almost tame in beginning a speech: sentence after sentence came out almost as it seemed involuntarily, but each contained a thought clearly expressed, each carried on the impression made by the last, each seemed to interest the speaker as well as his hearers, until he became animated by their increasing interest and pleasure, and brought out the main point with precision and effect. Then he would add to or elaborate it just enough to make sure of its being understood, and before passing on to the next subject would often pause and seem to ponder as he spoke, until of a sudden he looked up as if something had just struck him, made his next point with unfailing success, and sat down quickly after, leaving the audience surprised to find how short, how excellent, how complete was the speech. From this description it would appear that he was making up the speech as he went along and sometimes he did; but for important occasions he spent many hours and weeks preparing what he was to say and rehearsed his speech repeatedly so that often he would be able to deliver it without a text in front of him or even notes."

Writing

Most of Paget's legacies come to us through his writings and he produced over two hundred books and papers. Each shows the clarity of his thought and how clearly he had observed conditions which others had overlooked. Like all Victorians his sentences were long but, compared with many of his colleagues, he managed to write concisely and with purpose. In describing new conditions he managed to cover most of the facts and, in many cases, his descriptions could not be bettered today. This goes back to his days when cataloguing the specimens at the College of Surgeons. He would spend much time looking at the specimen and insist that what was written should cover exactly what was seen and that nothing should be surmised or added that was not there.

Paget as a man

Sir James Paget was a quiet, gentle, gracious and humble man. He was deeply religious and he rarely lost his temper. He was neat and tidy and was precise in everything that he did. He treated everyone with courtesy and tact and would listen intently before coming to a decision. If he had a fault it was that he did not like upsetting people and this led him in some committees to prolong discussions and delay making decisions. However, when he had made up his mind, or he thought a cause was just, he was prepared to stick to it. Even in old age he felt he had a disadvantage in not having had a classical education or not having gone to University, but this did not prevent him from mixing with all the top politicians, writers, scientists, artists and members of the Royal Family. Throughout his life he had a passionate desire to observe and to learn. He was a workaholic and loved it. As he said 'Work itself is a pleasure'.

James Paget University Hospital

The James Paget University Hospital replaced the Great Yarmouth General Hospital which Sir James opened in 1888. The new hospital opened to its first patients on 21 December 1981. It was built in two stages and eventually had over 500 beds. It is a 'Best Buy' designed District General Hospital providing care for a population of a quarter of a million people which expands by the influx of many visitors during the summer months.

When it was first opened at Gorleston-on-Sea on the east coast of Norfolk - half way between Great Yarmouth and Lowestoft - it was called the District General Hospital. Many names for it had been suggested such as Nelson, Lady Hamilton, Princess Diana and Prince William. In the end, the suggestion by Consultant Physician David Wayne to name it after Sir James Paget prevailed. The District Health Authority thought that by naming the hospital after a person who was born and grew up in Great Yarmouth, it would alienate those who lived in Lowestoft and Suffolk. They planned to name it after Prince William, the elder son of Prince Charles and Princess Diana. However, when it came to the vote James Paget was approved by eight votes to seven on 3 September 1984.

The hospital has been remarkably successful and the local population is very proud to have its own hospital. Through fund raising, the local people have been able to provide many facilities which other hospitals do not have. The hospital had the third CT Scanner in East Anglia after Addenbrooke's Hospital, Cambridge and Ipswich Hospital. An appeal for £370,000 was launched hoping to raise the amount within two years. Within six months £500,000 was raised. This was a Guinness World Record. An appeal started by Dr. David Wayne allowed a renal dialysis unit to be opened on 1 July 1991. £500,000 was raised by public appeal spearheaded by Dr. Terry Mitchell for out patient facilities and a lounge for people receiving chemotherapy. This was named after Sandra Chapman, Deaconess for Hopton and Corton who had suggested the scheme and it was opened in January 1992 by the Bishop of Norwich. Local appeals and legacies help to fund endoscopes and a new Endoscopic Unit. £150,000 was raised in 1993 to establish a Breast Care Unit and local appeals enabled the purchase of mammography screening vans. Further appeals allowed for the replacement of the old CT Scanner and the purchase of a MRI Scanner.

In 2000 an appeal was launched for £600,000 to fund the equipment for a new Intensive Care Ward costing £1,800,000. In the last six years £1,500,000 have been raised to fund the building of a Palliative Care Unit which provides advice and care for patients and their families with life limiting conditions. It also oversees the provision of palliative care facilities throughout the district and provides education and training.

Since the hospital became a NHS Trust in 1993 it has always balanced its books. It has benefitted from having good management and keen, enthusiastic clinicians and other health professionals as well as many dedicated staff. It was fortunate in having two excellent chief executives, Mike Pollard and David Hill, who were in post for a total of twelve years resulting in stability as well as advancement in services. They were backed up by John Wells as chairman, who served for over ten years. The Trust also helped to establish the Medical School at the University of East Anglia. Throughout this period the Trust met and exceeded all the targets and became the first Foundation Trust in Norfolk and Suffolk. It was renamed the James Paget University Hospitals NHS Foundation Trust in 2006.

Entrance to James Paget University Hospital

Unfortunately, a few years later the Care Quality Commission (CQC) found the Trust to be failing in a number of its standards. In spite of putting forward various action plans these were not effective and the Trust and its staff suffered at the hands of the media. This led to extremely low staff morale and subsequent visits by the CQC found further failings.

The problems were that the governance and reporting systems in the hospital were not fit for purpose. The Trust had a thorough governance review in 2011/12 which led to a strong action plan to facilitate the on-going improvements through 2012/13.

The concerns of staff and governors appeared not to have been listened to and certainly were not acted upon effectively enough. The hospital was not coping with increasing emergency admissions so that these patients were scattered all over the hospital, making medical and nursing care very difficult and resulting in the cancellation of many elective surgical operations.

Chairman John Hemming resigned to be replaced by Non Executive Director, Peter Franzen on an interim basis. Some months later Wendy Slaney retired as Chief Executive and David Hill, who had been running health services in Bermuda for five years, agreed to return as interim Chief Executive. He brought with him Tina Cookson as interim Director of Nursing; appointed Consultant Surgeon, John Studley as interim Medical Director and Claire Rooney as Director of Patient Flow.

There was a marked improvement in the processing of patients through the Accident and Emergency Department and the number of elective operations started to increase. The CQC returned for further inspections and within the year the hospital was found to be compliant in all measures. The improvements continued, performance was sustained and the Trust remains fully compliant following an inspection in February 2013. This was a staggering turnaround and speaks highly of the dedication and commitment of all staff. It also showed the importance of good leadership. Monitor, the regulator of Health Services, remarked that no Trust had ever turned around so quickly.

David Wright was appointed Chairman in June 2012, Christine Allen started as Chief Executive on 1 July 2013, Liz Libiszewski started as Director of Nursing, Quality and Patient Experience in August 2013 and Nick Oligbo has been Medical Director since April 2013.

In the last eighteen months the improvement in medical and nursing care has been remarkable and with it have been improvements in staff morale and a reduction in sick leave. The results of National patient and staff surveys show improvement in most parameters and the mortality rates put the Trust in the top thirteen trusts in the country.

Clinically, the hospital has frequently been a leader. It was the first hospital in East Anglia to provide a stoma care service and was one of the first hospitals in the country to pioneer patient controlled analgesia. At one time it had more Patient Controlled Analgesia Pumps than any other hospital, thanks to the generosity of the local population who funded them. These pumps enable patients to control their pain relief by pressing a button. For many years the hospital was the only hospital in East Anglia to provide mammography for NHS patients. The Pain Relief Clinic has a national and International reputation and the Retinal Screening Programme for diabetic patients was years ahead of its time when it was set up with public donations in 1987. Unfortunately, this service is no longer provided in house but by a national organisation.

The Audiology Department was one of only a few centres to assess digital hearing aids for NHS patients and has been involved in universal neonatal hearing screening since it was started. The Critical Care Score was developed here in the 1980s and now is standard practice in all hospitals nationally. It involves taking some basic observations and calculating a score which can indicate the early deterioration of a patient so that appropriate action may be taken.

Although the Breast Screening Service is one of the smallest units in the Eastern Region its results are usually in the top three in the Region. Professor Jerome Pereira started performing breast reconstructive surgery in the 1990s for breast cancer and, through his work, all hospitals in the country now participate in a national audit programme of which he is the National Clinical Lead. There are now three oncoplastic breast surgeons working in the hospital.

Charter marks were introduced by the John Major government to reward excellent service and these were awarded to the Tracheostomy Support Service, the Breast Nursing Service, the Children's Ward, the Day Case Eye Service and the Sandra Chapman Unit among others.

Over the years there has been an increasing investment in education and research. The Burrage Centre was built as the medical education, sports and social centre for the hospital and was largely financed by the benevolence of Mrs. Lily Burrage. It was opened in 1987 by Noel Johnson, Chairman of the District Health Authority. It ran independently from, but in close cooperation with, the Trust. Over the years it was a popular venue for social and sports activities and many educational programmes took place there. It was also enlarged several times with the finances coming from the revenue it generated. However, after over twenty years it suffered financial problems and it was agreed that the Trust would take it over. Since then it has been reconstructed to provide a re-designed educational centre containing the Sir James Paget Library - transferred from the main hospital - and the nucleus of the research department. It is sad that the sports and social centre is no longer there, although there is an area for refreshments and relaxation, and it is hoped that a group of staff will re-establish a social club.

The amount of research increases yearly way ahead of projections and the Trust is an active partner in training medical students from the University of East Anglia. This has led to having excellent junior doctors and the hope that many will be keen to settle in the area as general practitioners and hospital consultants. Sir James maintained his links with his students and it is to be hoped that his hospital will do the same with its students and young doctors.

With the development of e-learning Professor Jerome Pereira and Professor Sam Leinster, the first Dean of the Medical School, have devised and instituted postgraduate programmes for Breast Surgery, Colorectal Surgery and some anaesthetic and orthopaedic courses. Others are planned and Professor Pereira is lecturing on these programmes internationally. On 7 November 2013 the James Paget University Hospital, in association with the University of East Anglia, won the National Gold Award for the best online distance learning programme for their Masters of Surgery degree programmes in Oncoplastic Breast Surgery, gastroenterology and regional anaesthesia. This was a great achievement as the competition was open to Universities and big businesses throughout the United Kingdom and abroad.

A few years ago the hospital hit a bad patch but, thanks to the quality of its staff and present leadership, it is now going forwards. The National Health Service is under enormous pressures. Cost savings of £5-6,000,000 annually are required by the Trust and there are moves to take services into the community. It would provide much better seamless care if the Trust oversaw the community services as well.

This hospital has shown over the years that it is up to change. In many fields it has been a leader in innovation and it must continue to do so. Sir James emphasised the need to integrate science with practice and this is certainly being done. He showed the importance of hard work and looking at the whole patient in their management. 'The patient comes first' is part of the Trust's philosophy and it needs to adapt, as it has done in the past, to changing times. There are plans to develop a health campus on the site and it is important that this should go forward. Alongside this one must concentrate on providing excellent care at all times and combine this with first class training for all staff, including medical, nursing and other students, and expanding the research that is done here.

The hospital's greatest asset is its staff. They need to be supported and encouraged and, given the right leadership and incentives, the future could be bright. In the present national financial and NHS climate this may appear over-optimistic but perhaps it is worth remembering the example of Sir James Paget. He had little money and no backing yet, by shear hard work and determination, he was able to succeed to become the father of British Pathology, a great Physiologist, a superb teacher, a first class clinician, a wonderful writer and orator, President of the Royal College of Surgeons and Surgeon to Queen Victoria. The challenge is there for all members of the James Paget University Hospital.

Paget's other connections.

Several organisations, clubs and parts of buildings have been named after him. St. Bartholomew's Hospital still has the Paget ward. The James Paget University Hospital has the Sir James Paget Library. It also has the Paget Club which was formed over ten years ago to provide a forum for junior doctors to deliver papers in the presence of their peers and seniors. Each doctor has ten minutes in which to present a paper and answer questions. The papers are marked by a group of consultants and there is a monetary prize for the best presentation. Following the presentations a consultant used to give a talk and the evening ended with a buffet supper. Unfortunately, because of the difficulties in financing the meals and the fact that many junior doctors live in Norwich, it was decided to stop the evening meetings and to hold the Paget Club presentations at several of the Grand Rounds throughout the year which are held at lunchtime.

The Paget's Association was founded in 1973 by Ann Stansfield MBE. The charity is based in Manchester and provides information and support to those with Paget's Disease of Bone, to raise awareness of the disease among health professionals and the general public and to sponsor research in the causes and treatment of the condition.

The Paget Foundation is based in Brooklyn, New York and provides information for patients, health professionals and researchers about Paget's disease of Bone.

The Sir James Paget Room in British Medical Association House in London provides a fine dining room for 120 people and can be combined with the John Snow Room to form the Lutyens Suite which seats 220 people. Sir Edwin Lutyens was the architect of the building which the BMA bought in 1925.

Main Writings of Sir James Paget

1834 *Sketch of the Natural History of Yarmouth and its Neighbourhood.* By CJ and James Paget. K.Skill: Yarmouth. Pp.88

1835 *Account of the Trichina Spiralis.* Trans. Abernethian Society.

1840 *On White Spots on the surface of the Heart, and on the frequency of Pericarditis.* Trans. Med. Chir. Soc., xxiii. 29.

1842 *On the chief results obtained by the use of the Microscope in the study of Human Anatomy and Physiology.* British and Foreign Medical Review.
On the relation between the Symmetry and the Disease of the Body.
Trans. Med. Chir. Soc., xxv. 30.

1844 *Report on the Progress of Human Anatomy and Physiology in the year 1842-3.*
British and Foreign Medical Review.
On obstructions of the Branches of the Pulmonary Artery.
Trans. Med. Chir. Soc., xxvii. 162
Examination of a Cyst containing seminal fluid.
Trans. Med. Chir. Soc., xxvii. 398.

1845 *Report on the Progress of Human Anatomy and Physiology in the year 1843-4.*
British and Foreign Medical Review.
Address at the Abernethian Society (Fiftieth Session).
Additional Observations on Obstructions of the Pulmonary Arteries.
Trans. Med. Chi. Soc., xxviii.353.

1846 *Catalogue of the Pathological Specimens in the Museum of St. Bartholomew's Hospital.* Pp487.
First Volume of the Pathological Catalogue of the College of Surgeons Museum. Pp. 144.
Report on the Progress of Human Anatomy and

Physiology during the year 1844-5. British and Foreign Medical Review.
Records of Harvey, in extracts from the Journals of the Royal Hospital of St. Bartholomew. London: John Churchill. Pp. 37. (Reprinted in the St. Bartholomew's Hospital Reports, xxii. 1886)
On the Motives to Industry in the Study of Medicine: an address at the opening of the Hospital-sessions, October, 1846.
Account of a case in which the corpus callosum, fornix, and septum lucidum were imperfectly formed. Trans. Med. Chir. Soc., xxix. 55.

1847 *Second Volume of the College Catalogues.* Pp. 225.
Lectures on Nutrition (Arris and Gale Lectures). Med. Times.

1848 *Third Volume of the College Catalogue.* Pp.287.
Handbook of Physiology. By William Senhouse Kirkes and James Paget
Lectures on the Life of the Blood (Arris and Gale Lectures). Med. Times.
Account of a dislocation in consequence of disease of the first and second cervical vertebrae.
Trans. Med. Chir. Soc., xxxi. 285.

1849 *Fourth and Fifth Volumes of the College Catalogue.* Pp. 350+182
Lectures on the Process of Repair and Reproduction after Injury (Arris and Gale Lectures).Med. Times.

1850 *Lectures on Inflammation* (Arris and Gales Lectures). Med. Times.
On the Freezing of the Albumen of Eggs. Phil. Trans. Roy. Soc.
On Fatty Degeneration of the Small Blood-vessels of he Brain, and its relation to Apoplexy.

Trans. Abern. Soc.
A case of Aneurismal Dilatation of the Popliteal Artery, treated with Pressure.
Trans. Abern. Soc.

1851 *Lectures on Tumours* (Arris and Gale Lectures). Med. Times and Gazette.
On the Recent Progress of Anatomy, and its influence on Surgery. A Lecture at the College of Surgeons, July 2. Med. Times and Gazette.

1852 *Lectures on Malignant Tumours* (Arris and Gale Lectures). Med. Times and Gazette.

1853 *First Edition of Lectures on Surgical Pathology: being the Arris and Gale Lectures, with additions. T*wo volumes. Pp 499+637. Longmans.
Two cases of inguinal hernia, in which the sac was pushed back with the intestines.
Med. Times and Gazette.

1854 *On the importance of the study of Physiology, as a branch of education for all classes.*
Lecture at the Royal Institution, June.
Account of a growth of cartilage in a testicle and its lymphatics, and in other parts.
Trans. Med. Chir. Soc., xxxviii. 247.

1856 *The Physiognomy of the Human Mind.*
Quarterly Review, September.

1857 *On the Cause of the Rhythmic Motion of the Heart:* the Croonian Lecture. Proc. Roy. Soc.
On the hereditary transmission of tendencies to cancerous and other tumours.
Med. Times and Gazette.
Account of a case in which the administration of chloroform was fatal.
Med.Times and Gazette.

1859 *The Chronometry of Life:* A Lecture at the Royal Institution. Med. Times and Gazette.

1860 *Articles in Holmes's System of Surgery.*

1862 *On the treatment of patients after surgical*

       operations: the Address in Surgery at the annual meeting of the British Medical Association. Med. Times and Gazette.
1863 *Second Edition* (with Sir W. Turner) *of the Lectures on Surgical Pathology.*
       Introductory Address at the opening of the Hospital session. Lancet, ii..
1864 *Scarlet fever after operations.* BMJ, ii. 1864.
1865 *Inaugural Address at the opening of the new buildings of the Leeds School of Medicine.*
       Cases of Chronic Pyaemia. St. Bartholomew's Hospital Reports, i. 1.
1866 *Gouty and some forms of Phlebitis.* St. B.H. Reports, ii. 82.
1867 *Senile Scrofula.* St. B.H. Reports, iii. 412.
       The Various Risks of Operations. Lancet, ii.
       Causes that Bonesetters cure. BMJ, ii. 1.
1868 *The Calamities of Surgery:* a clinical lecture.
       Stammering with other organs than those of speech. BMJ., ii.
1869 *Presidential Address to the Clinical Society of London.*
       What becomes of Medical Students. St. B.H. Reports, v. 238.
       Residual Abscesses. St. B.H. Reports, v. 73
       Treatment of Carbuncle. Lancet, i.
       A case of suppression of urine very slowly fatal. Trans Clin. Soc., ii.
1870 *Third Edition of the Lectures on Surgical Pathology.*
       Sexual Hypochondriasis: a clinical lecture.
       The production of some of the loose bodies in joints. St. B.H. Reports, vi. 1.
       Cancer following ichthyosis of the tongue. Clin. Soc. iii.
       Necrosis of the femur without external inflammation. Clin. Soc. iii.
       Wasting of part of the tongue in connection with disease of the occipital bone. Clin. Soc.

1871 *On dissection-wounds.* Lancet, i.
Cancerous tumours of bone. Trans.
Trans. Med. Chir. Soc.,liv.
A case illustrating certain nervous disorders.
St. B. H. Reports, vii.67.
1872 *Lectures on Strangulated Hernia.*
BMJ., i. and ii.
1873 *Memoir of William and Edward Ormerod.*
St. B. H. Reports, ix.
Lectures on Nervous Mimicry. Lancet, ii.
1874 *Disease of the Mammary Areola preceding Cancer of the Gland.* St. B. H. Reports, x. 87.
Presidential Address in the Section of Surgery, Annual meeting of the British Medical Association. BMJ., ii.
Remarks on Pyaemia. Trans. Clin. Soc., vii.
Remarks on Cancer. Trans. Clin. Soc., xxv.
1875 *First Edition of Clinical Lectures and essays.* Edited with notes by Mr. Howard Marsh. Longmans.
1876 *Fourth Edition of the Lectures on Surgical Pathology.*
On a form of chronic inflammation of the bones (osteitis deformans). Trans. Med. Chir. Soc. lx.
On some of the sequels of Typhoid Fever.
St. B.H. Reports, xii.1.
On certain points in the pathology of Syphilis. BMJ, i.
Presidential Address to the Royal Medical and Chirurgical Society of London. BMJ.
1877 *Hunterian Oration.* BMJ., i.
Presidential Address, Roy. Med. Chir. Society.
Cases of Branchial Fistulae in the External Ears. Trans. Med. Chir. Soc., lxi.
1878 *On Indurations of the Breast becoming cancerous.* St. B. H. Reports, xiv. 65
The Contrast of Temperance with Abstinence. Contemporary Review, November.
1879 *Second Edition of the Clinical Lectures and*

Essays; including four lectures on Gout in some of its surgical relations.
Memoir of George William Callender.
St. B. H. Reports xv.
Anaesthetics: the History of a Discovery.
Nineteenth Century.
Case of polypi of the antrum.
Trans. Clin. Soc., xii.

1880 *Elemental Pathology: the Presidential Address in the Section of Pathology, at the annual meeting of the British Medical Association.* BMJ, ii.
Suggestions for the making of Pathological Catalogues. BMJ, ii.
Theology and Science: an address at the Leeds Clergy School, December, 1880

1881 *Presidential Address at the International Medical Congress in London.*
The Vivisection Question. Nineteenth Century.
First Volume of the new edition of the College Catalogue (With Dr. Goodhart and Mr. Alban Doran).

1882 *On some Rare and New diseases: the Bradshawe Lecture at the College of Surgeons.* BMJ, ii.
Notes on seven additional cases of Osteitis Deformans. Trans. Med. Chir. Soc., lxv.

1883 *Third Volume of the new edition of the College Catalogue.*
On *the National Value of Public Health: an address in connection with the International Health Exhibition.* BMJ, i.

1885 *Fourth Volume of the new edition of the College Catalogue.*
Remarks on Charcot's Disease.
Trans. Clin. Soc., xviii.
An address at Netley Hospital, at the presentation of prizes.
St. Bartholomew's Hospital and School, fifty

years ago: an address to the Abernethian Society. BMJ, i.

1886 *An address at Oxford, on the unveiling of John Hunter's statue in the University Museum.* BMJ, ii.

1887 *On Cancer and Cancerous Diseases: the Morton Lecture at the College of Surgeons.* BMJ, ii. 1887.
On the Future of Pathology: Presidential Address to the Pathological Society of London. Trans. Path. Soc. xxxviii.
Report on Charcot's Disease (with other members of the Clinical Society's Committee). Trans. Clin. Soc., xx.
Report of the Pasteur Commission (with Mr. Victor Horsley).
On the utility of scientific work in practice: an introductory address at Owens College. BMJ, ii.
Memoir of Sir George Burrow. St. B. H. Reports, xxiii.

1888 *Address to London University Extension Students.*

1889 *Address at the Mansion House meeting in recognition of the Pasteur treatment against rabies.*

1890 *Address at University College, Liverpool.*

1891 *Studies of Old Case-books: seventeen essays on subjects in surgical pathology and practice.* Longmans. Pp 168.
A short account of Mr. Pasteur's work. Nature.
A short paper in the Virchow Festschrift.

1894 *An address to the Abernethian Society, at the beginning of its hundredth session.* BMJ, ii.

SYNOPSES of TALKS to be GIVEN at PAGET BICENTENARY CONFERENCE

To celebrate James Paget's life, his many achievements and the influence he has had on so many aspects of life an all day conference is to be held at the James Paget University Hospital on Saturday 11 January 2014. Synopses of many of these talks are given below.

Sir James Paget – Surgeon Extraordinary

Hugh Sturzaker
Retired Surgeon, James Paget University Hospital
Lead Governor, James Paget University Hospital

This talk will cover the life of Sir James, his many achievements and his legacies. A synopsis is not given here as details are covered in this book.

James Paget's contribution to breast disease and major milestones leading to the evolution of a new specialty

Dick Rainsbury

Consultant Oncoplastic Surgeon, Royal Hampshire County Hospital, Winchester
President of Association of Breast Surgery (2011-2013)

James Paget's celebrated paper linking nipple changes to underlying breast cancer was published 150 years ago. His beautifully perceptive description of the disease has stood the test of time, reflecting a gift for observation and attention to detail which is clearly evident in his early sketches of Great Yarmouth. The origin of the Paget cell has been fiercely debated ever since - as has the most effective treatment of the disease. Something which he would have greatly relished!

Much has happened in the interim, with the management of breast cancer changing beyond recognition. Radical surgery has been replaced by multimodal treatment, as the responsibility for breast cancer patients has passed from the hands of the generalist to the hands of the multidisciplinary specialist team. Cross-specialty education and training has increased to keep pace with patient-led demand for surgeons with a full range of oncoplastic skills. And as breast surgery moves further away from general surgery, the rationale for specialty recognition continues to grow.

Past, present and future: Evidence-based practice in reconstructive breast surgery

Sue Down
Consultant Oncoplastic Breast Surgeon, James Paget University Hospital
Honorary Senior Lecturer, University of East Anglia

Sir James Paget excelled in observational analysis and practical application of his findings. His early work on the pathology of trichinosis resulted in improved public health outcomes though clinical education.

These principles of data collection, interpretation and clinical application are demonstrated in a recent national breast audit which has its origins at the James Paget University Hospital. The National Mastectomy and Breast Reconstruction Audit (NMBRA) has set new standards for reconstructive breast surgery through the publication of national guidelines for best practice in oncoplastic breast surgery.

The NMBRA started as a local audit in the 1990s, conducted by Professor Jerome Pereira, a consultant breast surgeon at the James Paget University Hospital. He analysed his operative outcomes, and the experiences and opinions of his patients regarding their cosmetic results following surgery. At this time, breast reconstruction was not widely practiced, and was only available to approximately 7% of women undergoing mastectomy for breast cancer.

Professor Pereira's work led to the successful East Anglian Breast Audit, analysing local breast units' outcomes. With the support of the Association of Breast Surgery (ABS) and Royal

College of Surgeons of England, and in association with the British Association of Plastic, Reconstructive and Aesthetic Surgeons (BAPRAS), the NMBRA was developed and launched in January 2008.The audit ran over 15 months, and collected data from both clinicians and patients regarding all mastectomy cases with or without breast reconstruction.

The study analysed the provision and outcomes of mastectomy and breast reconstruction surgery for women in England and Wales. It is the largest audit of patient outcomes worldwide, with participation by 100% of NHS Trusts, including over 18,000 women. Four annual reports have been produced, detailing the local provision of breast reconstruction services, analysing outcomes by type of reconstruction, describing complications following breast reconstruction, and providing patient related outcome measures (PROMS). Key recommendations from the annual NMBRA reports have informed the 2009 National Institute for Health and Care Excellence (NICE) guidelines, and recent 2012 ABS/ BAPRAS publication, Oncoplastic Breast Reconstruction: Guidelines for Best Practice.

Work is continuing to build on the findings of the NMBRA, with 5 year analysis of patient related outcomes measures to start shortly. There is no doubt that the NMBRA has improved the provision and quality of UK breast reconstructive surgery, and encouraged clinicians to reflect on and improve their individual outcome data.

So, what of the future? Work is on-going at the James Paget University Hospital to establish research protocols and audits to analyse and improve our clinical practice and patient outcomes. We continue to follow Sir James's example of founding our surgical practice in science.

References:

Breast Cancer: (early & locally advanced): diagnosis and treatment. NICE guideline CG80, February 2009

Oncoplastic Breast Reconstruction: Guidelines for Best Practice. Association of Breast Surgery, November 2012

Rejuvenate: A Moving-on Programme designed for women following breast cancer treatment.

Karen Flores
Breast Care Nurse Specialist, James Paget University Hospital

In 2010 the James Paget University Hospital advertised funding for nurses, calling for proposals and ideas to improve treatment for patients, relatives or staff. This project was called Innovations in Nursing and Midwifery Practice Project (INMPP).

The Breast Care Nurses wanted to provide a service for women after breast cancer treatment at our hospital. This inspiration followed after reading documents from the Department of Health on cancer survivorship and work from Professor Lesley Fallowfield. We felt our patients were missing out!

Our main concern was how we could fund such a project. We applied to the INMPP submitting the idea of our proposed project, and it was accepted.

We wanted to evaluate the effectiveness of a structured program which consisted of an education element; relaxation and complementary therapies; combined with a safe, individually designed exercise plan. We wanted to assess how each component of the program affected the health and well being of our patients.

Each patient entering the study was offered:

a. Three education sessions which took place at monthly intervals and consisted of an hour-long talk led by Breast Care Nurses and other healthcare professionals covering topics such as healthy eating plans, lymphoedema awareness and coping with treatment induced menopausal symptoms.
b. Ten individually designed gym sessions or a home based workout programme which were designed taking into account individual requirements.
c. All patients had the opportunity to attend yoga sessions and a taster Complementary Therapy session. This included:

- An Indian head massage
- A facial
- Body massage
- Make up session

A Breast Care Nurse facilitated each session. We encouraged our voluntary support group members to be present: Be Re Assured Scheme (BRAS) and Breast friends. We gave information leaflets covering topics we had discussed. The information included moving on after breast cancer and managing the financial implications.

136 patients were invited into the study. This took place at the James Paget University Hospital Trust, using the facilities and the hospital gym.

Patients were invited into the study by a Breast Care Nurse and we collected the following data:

- Demographics
- Adjuvant treatments
- Medical History
- Age

- Exercise History
- Medication
- At the gym induction we collected Body Mass Index, Blood Pressure and weight.

Before the programme we asked all patients to score how they perceived their general fitness, physical and emotional health using a Visual Analogue Scale (VAS). We reassessed this again at the end of the programme.

The project was over a twelve month period and each programme was three months in duration.

All sessions were well attended. We found the lymphoedema talk had the highest attendance which resulted in an increase to our lymphoedema service by 25%.

Conclusion

We found the programme had a positive impact on the general well being of women. However the exercise component was very expensive.

Patients enjoyed the companionship and the subject matter.

As a result of this study our programme has developed. We now run it over a 6 month period and prepare women for life after breast cancer. We encourage talking about fears and feelings. We have interactive sessions on motivation and confidence and a local college provides feel-good sessions in which students also attend.

We feel that we may be able to do a further study on the impact of the programme on long term survival. The benefits are two fold: patients enjoy it and the staff are able to see patients moving on from their breast cancer in a positive way.

Quotes from our patients:

"Its nice to meet people like me....... I am not so alone."

"The whole idea is brilliant! After a year of treatment it is easy to feel thrown out on your own when it finishes. The major advantage is meeting and talking to others who have been through the same experience."

"Thank you to all concerned with particular thanks to the ladies who have been through it themselves. They were inspiring."

"It was good to meet others and listen to their experiences. Everyone was so positive and cheerful. Some of us didn't want the sessions to end. Thank you to all involved."

REJUVENATE
A MOVING-ON PROGRAMME POST BREAST CANCER TREATMENT

Complementary Therapies Demonstrated by Lowestoft College

~ Reflexology

~ Crystals

~ Colour Therapy

~ Aromatherapy

~ Skin & Hair Care

~ Make Up

Relaxation Classes

Advice on:

~ Lymphoedema

~ Lingerie

~ Menopausal Symptoms

~ Confidence & Motivation

~ Healthy Lifestyle

This is a great way to meet other ladies and support each other alongside the breast care nurses and support groups.

James Paget University Hospitals NHS
NHS Foundation Trust

Paget and Medical Education

Chris McManus
*Professor of Psychology and Medical Education
University College London*

Sir James Paget not only described his eponymous diseases of bone and of nipple, identified the pork parasite *Trichinella spirali* while still a student, was a gifted surgeon and a President of the Royal College of Surgeons of England, and was an orator who impressed the young William Osler with his, "beautiful thoughts, clothed in the choicest words", but he also carried out the first formal studies of medical education. In its five pages, Paget's 1869 paper anticipates many modern approaches to research in medical education, and initiated the discipline as a science based on the statistical analysis of empirical data and rooted in psychological concepts.

The 1869 paper. The 1869 paper [1], which the Lancet described as "a brief but brilliant article" [2], starts with an anecdote about John Abernethy, the surgeon and teacher at St. Bartholomew's Hospital, whom Paget later said should be remembered "as a man of rare sagacity [and] an admirable surgeon and teacher". When entering a lecture theatre at the beginning of a session, Abernethy apparently said, "Good God! What will become of you?". It was that fundamental question which Paget set out to answer, as he put it, "in the dullest way – by statistics" [3].

Paget was appointed to St. Bartholomew's Hospital in 1839 as Warden of the College, and lectured on Morbid Anatomy from 1839 to 1843, and on Physiology and General and Morbid Anatomy from 1843 to 1859. The 1869 paper is based on his 'entry-book', which recorded the students registering for his courses, the paper studying the conveniently round number of 1000 (out of 1325) of the students who could be traced by him and his collaborators. A strikingly modern feature of the paper is the use of behaviourally anchored outcomes for describing the careers, with clear definitions of 'Distinguished success', 'Great success' through to 'Limited success' and 'Failed entirely', the latter including William Palmer, the Rugeley Poisoner, who in 1856 was hanged for murder. The use of behavioural anchors probably derived from Paget's philosophy, developed while cataloguing the pathological collections of Bart's and the College of Surgeons, that "nothing was to be told but what was there and could be seen".

The entry-book. Paget's entry-book is preserved in the library of the Royal College of Surgeons of England in London [4]. The original register with its very pale green pages was later interleaved with pages of a medium blue and rebound. Paget used the new pages to write brief descriptions of the careers of 386 of the 1325 entrants, the other students presumably being classified by his collaborators at Bart's, Sir Thomas Smith (1833-1909) and George William Callender (1830-78). Paget's own comments, which show his intense interest in teaching and in his students, are rich, varied, witty and sometimes filled with pathos, providing still a panoply of the highlights and lowlife of Victorian medicine.

> **Jonathan Hutchinson:** "One of the most industrious observers of cases that I ever knew. I recommended him for the work of reporting for the Medical Gazette, & he did excellently in it & rose well."

> **Dr Elizabeth Blackwell:** "The celebrated Dr. Elizabeth Blackwell – a sensible, quiet, discreet lady, – she gained a fair knowledge (not more) of medicine;

practised in New York; then tried to promote female doctordom in England."

E.L. LaFargue: "Loitered about as a student; & being rather pretty & having a little money, he left in 1854-55 & slowly qualified for the Army. Was to have his commission in 1860, but he joined Garibaldi."

Clement John Carnell: "Stupid, dissolute, drunken. After he passed, a woman whom he lived with being pregnant, he killed her by the ignorant way in which he tried to produce abortion & he then committed suicide. He was much under the guidance of Sievier – Aug '59."

James Richard Hancorn: "Idle, dissipated, drinking, – associate of Sievier. Had to resign the House Surgeoncy; practised a few months with his father in Shoreditch; & died in 1860."

Tom Oliver Hunt: "Good tempered, easy, rather careless. Was an assistant variously; but in 1861 was drinking hard & fast losing way."

F.W. Brown: "Idle and dissipated, but pulled up in time & was in fair prospects at Uppingham in 1864."

George Taylor: "Unteachably dull, though willing & with no vice. He could get no diploma, but went to be an assistant to his brother in Essex & was 'very well liked'."

Joseph Eld: "One of the most laborious, clear-headed, and capacious students I ever knew. He could learn everything without a fault. Besides, he was eminently industrious & gentle. So beautiful a mind, surely never occupied so grotesque & strange a body: and this inferior part of him died after his 2nd year of study."

Psychological observations. Paget's early academic reputation was from cataloguing pathological collections, and his study of medical students is perhaps another "love of index-making", with the 1869 paper being a cataloguing of souls rather than specimens. George Eliot's dictum in *Middlemarch,* that, "a medical man likes to make psychological observations", was undoubtedly true of Paget, who ends the 1869 paper by saying that, "in watching and reflecting on the careers of my pupils, I have come to some strong beliefs on medical education":

> "the personal character, the very nature, the will, of each student had far greater force in determining his career than any helps or hindrances whatever."

Elsewhere he put it more pithily: "Such as the student had been, such was the practitioner", although, "There were some few exceptions..." Elsewhere he asks, "What is to be the driving force?", and concludes "It must be each man's will, by whatever motive stirred; when the will is wanting, the most perfect scheme is useless."

Paget's achievements in medical education research. Paget's great achievements in his prescient 1869 paper can be summarised in modern terms:

- A longitudinal study of a large and complete cohort of students, including the failures as well as the successes;
- Clear outcome measures which are behaviourally anchored;

- Statistical analysis in the comparison of groups of students;

- Interpretation of individual differences in terms of personality and motivation.

It was to be nearly a century before medical education researchers again attempted such studies.

References

1. Paget J: *What becomes of medical students.* Saint Bartholomew's Hospital Reports 1869;**5**: 238-242.

2. Anonymous.: *"What becomes of medical students?".* Lancet 1869, **ii**: 653-654.

3. Paget S: *Memoirs and letters of Sir James Paget, edited by Stephen Paget.* London: Longmans, Green and Co; 1901.

4. McManus IC: *Sir James Paget's research on medical education.* Lancet 2005, **366**: 506-513.

Are we making Doctors fit for the 21st Century?

Professor David Crossman
Dean of the Medical School, University of East Anglia
Honorary Consultant Cardiologist, Norfolk and Norwich University Hospital.

This paper will discuss the establishment of the Medical School at the University of East Anglia and the ways medical education must adapt to prepare young doctors for the continued evolution of medical practice.

Sir James Paget and his influence on Postgraduate Medical Education.

Professor Jerome Pereira
Consultant Surgeon at James Paget University Hospital
Senior Lecturer at the University of East Anglia

Sir James Paget was a renowned teacher and reformer in medial education in the latter half of the nineteenth century, and his influence in these areas continues to this day.

James Paget began his surgical career as an apprentice to Mr. Charles Costerton, his family doctor and a surgeon in Great Yarmouth for nearly five years. He then went on to complete his further training at St. Bartholomew's Medical School, London.

From Sir James Paget's day the apprenticeship model of surgical education was alive and well until Calman training was established fifteen years ago. More recently the European Working Time Directive has limited doctors to 48-hours working and has had a negative impact on education and training. More than two-thirds of colorectal and breast trainees surveyed are dissatisfied with the current training programmes, confirming the results of previous surveys conducted among surgical trainees.

Surgical educators and trainees require a new mindset to meet current education training needs.

Medical education has undergone major changes with increasing understanding of cognitive psychology and leading to new theories of learning, particularly among adult learners.

The use of new technologies, including e-Learning and simulation, add rich values to the educational process. The problem-based learning approach and small group learning have enabled student directed learning and strengthened evidence-based practice. The explosion of medical knowledge demands that students are trained in critical evaluation for application of new knowledge to clinical practice.

The exciting new development of blended learning, uses lessons learnt from the apprentice model and incorporates new educational strategies and technology like e-Learning, simulation and development of professional and critical evaluational skills to improve the overall experience of learning and the quality of education to a new generation of trainees. The University of East Anglia Mastership in Oncoplastic Breast Surgery embodies the best in blended learning, is the highest qualification in the UK for breast specialists and is recognised internationally. The success of this initiative has extended to development and delivery of Masterships in colorectal surgery, regional anaesthesia and knee surgery.

PATHOLOGY: FROM PAGET to the PRESENT DAY

Dr. Mark Wilkinson,
Consultant Histopathologist, Norfolk and Norwich University Hospital
Senior Lecturer at University of East Anglia

James Paget was one of the earliest "proper" pathologists; someone who sought to explain the links between the symptoms he and his peers recognised as the indicators of a disease and the process that caused the disease itself. His seminal paper on the ailment which became known as Paget's disease of bone was entitled *On a form of chronic inflammation of bones*. It demonstrates this desire to understand and explain the mechanism of disease (In modern pathology we would probably not classify Paget's disease as an inflammatory condition).

Sir James identified an unusual pattern of eczematous change around the nipple as being an early feature of breast cancer. This has become the second most well known disease which bears his name: Paget's disease of the breast. By meticulous recording of the course of the disease he was able to correctly surmise that it was an early manifestation of the disease. The clarity and precision of Paget's original description led to a wide dissemination of his work, allowing others to take his observations as their starting point and move our knowledge and understanding a step forward. This is perhaps the hallmark of modern science (pathological and otherwise).

As pathology evolved over the subsequent two centuries it has used this basic scientific skill of accurate observation and precise recording to identify avenues to explore by more technically demanding means.

In the case of Paget's disease of breast the development of modern microscopes and staining with the then common clothes dyes let the earlier pathologists recognise the presence of an abnormal population of cells in the upper layers of the skin (epidermis). Other physicians and pathologists were able to recognise a similar phenomenon at other sites so leading to other diseases collectively called extra mammary Paget's. This led to a further exploration of the process and recognition, that in all cases, the disease was believed to be an extension of cancer cells into the epidermis, a feature now called Pagetoid spread.

In the late twentieth century further developments allowed pathologists to stain to identify particular proteins on cells. Thus in the case of mammary Paget's disease staining for a specific molecule shows the infiltrating cells in brown, where their normal neighbours are not stained confirming the belief that the "Paget's cells" are a discreet population with differing phenotype (appearance and protein structure) from their neighbours, thus supporting the infiltration hypothesis.

Rare cases of Paget's with no underlying cancer were difficult to explain, but the possibility that the "primary" tumour was within the intra epidermal portion of the breast duct seemed likely.

Further technical developments in pathological science have allowed identification of individual gene mutations in diseased cells. Thus, we are able to recognise that in some cases of Paget's disease the Paget cells are genetically different from the underlying tumour in as many as 20% of cases, so leading to a recognition that the phenomenon is one of infiltration of the skin by tumour cells, but not invariably those originating outside the skin itself.

These developments in scientific understanding are not merely of interest, they lead to real improvements in patient care. In the early days, Paget's recognition that a rare pattern of eczema resistant to the normal treatments was an early indicator of developing breast cancer would have led to earlier surgery and thus a greater chance of cure. In modern times, the exploration of the genotype of malignant cells opens up whole new avenues of potential for developing new and effective treatments often based on drugs rather than surgery. The now standard use of Herceptin as a drug to treat patients whose breast cancer bears the HER2 mutation indicates how far pathological science has come standing on the shoulders of giants such as Sir James Paget.

References:

Paget, J. *On a form of chronic inflammation of bones (osteitis deformans)*. Trans Med-Chir Soc, 1877; **60**:37-40.

Paget, J. *On disease of the mammary areola preceding cancer of the mammary gland.* St Bartholomew's Hosp. Rep. 1874; **10**:87-90.

Porter, C.B. *A Disease of the Mammary Areola Preceding Cancer of the Mammary Glands, Paget's Disease* Boston Med Surg J 1882; **106**:412-414.

Morandi, L. Pession, A et al. *Intraepidermal cells of Paget's carcinoma of the breast can be genetically different from those of the underlying carcinoma.* Human Pathology, 2003; **34**, Issue 12:1321–1330.

SIR JAMES PAGET - THE BICENTENARY OF HIS BIRTH

Professor Harold Ellis CBE, FRCS,
Emeritus Professor of Surgery, University of London.
Department of Anatomy, Guy's Hospital.

This year, 2014, marks the two-hundredth anniversary of the birth of Great Yarmouth's most famous doctor, James Paget, who was born on January 11, 1814, the son of a local merchant. He was to achieve a distinction as a shrewd clinical observer, an expert in surgical pathology and as a brilliant teacher. He is remembered eponymously in Paget's disease of bone, of the nipple and of the penis, as well as contributing to the recognition of several other pathologies.

James, like his six brothers, (one of whom, George, became Regius Professor of Medicine at Cambridge), went to school in Yarmouth. By the time he was 13, his father's business failed and the family fell on hard times. In 1830, James was apprenticed to Mr Charles Costerton, a Yarmouth apothecary. As well as learning to dispense, apply leeches and how to bleed his patients, James dissected, amputated limbs and studied the skeleton. He also became an expert on the botany and insect life of the region. In 1834 Paget entered as a medical student at St Bartholomew's Medical School, sharing lodgings with his brother George. In his very first year in the dissecting room, Paget made his first original observation. Tiny boney spicules were commonly observed in the muscles of the dissecting room cadavers, but had never been investigated. There were no microscopes at Bart's (!), but Paget obtained the use of one in the botanical department of the British Museum; each speck contained a tiny worm, *trichina spiralis*, coiled up within its capsule. Paget qualified MRCS in 1836.

Over the next years, the young surgeon, with no private means, earned a living by coaching medical students, as sub-editor of the "Medical Gazette", as curator of the Pathological Museum at Bart's (the salary was £40 a year), lecturing in pathology and engaging in a miniscule consulting practice. He spent seven years writing a catalogue of the Museum, with a detailed account of what could be seen, naked eye, in each specimen.

In 1843 Paget was appointed lecturer in physiology at the medical school and, at last, in 1847, at the age of 33, he was made assistant surgeon. He became full surgeon at Bart's in 1861.

Paget built up an enormous consulting practice. His deep knowledge of pathology led to his advice being sought about rare and difficult problems. Average working day would be 16 hours long, with much to do on Sundays, and with frequent long journeys, in those days by train, to see patients in different parts of the country. For 41 years he was surgeon to Queen Victoria and 36 years to Edward Prince of Wales.

James Paget died on December 30, 1899, within a few days of his 86th birthday.

But what of his eponyms?

Paget's disease of bone. In 1877, Paget published his account in Medico-Chirurgical Transactions of a 68-year-old man whom he had long observed with what he termed 'osteitis deformans'. He referred to four other patients and to three similar reports in the literature, one by Sir Samuel Wilks of Guy's Hospital eight years previously. Paget referred to this condition in two further papers and, after his original patient's death, presented photographs of the patient together with the main bones affected to the pathology museum at Bart's. This common condition remains as much a mystery regarding aetiology as it did in Paget's time.

Paget's Disease of the Nipple. In 1874, (*St Bartholomew's Reports*) Paget recorded 15 examples of 'certain chronic affections of the skin of the nipple and areola very often succeeded by the formation of scirrhous cancer in the mammary gland'. He did not describe the microscopic appearances of the condition, which were later recorded by one of his house surgeons and later successor on the staff at Bart's, Sir Henry Butlin. It is now recognised that this condition is due to a slowly growing duct carcinoma of the breast that infiltrates into the nipple.

Disease of the penis. In Paget's paper on the nipple lesions, he notes "I have seen a persistent rawness of the glans penis like a long enduring balanitis, followed, after more than a year's duration by cancer of the substance of the glans". This unusual lesion, (I have personally dealt with but a single case), is more commonly named the 'erythroplasia of Queyrat', described in 1911.

Several other rarities were described by Paget, including spontaneous or traumatic thrombosis of the axillary vein, first described by him in 1858. This patient was a 27 year old soldier, who made a complete recovery. He recorded (1853) two examples of subcutaneous tumours of the lower abdominal wall in women, ('Paget's recurring fibroid'), and noted two examples and one specimen of what he termed 'quiet necrosis of bone' (1870 and 1875) in what is now termed osteochondritis dessicans. Dr Batty Shaw, indeed, quotes eight lesions which were first recorded by Paget (Batty Shaw 1980).

It is hardly surprising that the title of Paget's Bradshaw lecture at the Royal College of Surgeons in 1882 was entitled 'New and Rare Diseases'!

What a remarkable clinical observer! Yarmouth can indeed be proud of its famous son!

Reference:

Batty Shaw A. (1980) Practitioner 224; 1323-7 'Paget's diseases' (This paper give references to the lesions which bear Paget's name)

Paget's Disease of Bone

Professor William D. Fraser
Professor of Medicine, Norwich Medical School
University of East Anglia

Sir James Paget first published the Clinical and Gross Pathological features of Paget's Disease of Bone in 1877 (Medical Chirurgical Transactions). The description of the first case in the Journal is as applicable and accurate today as it was when first published describing the significant signs and symptoms of Paget's disease from lateral bowing of the lower limbs, to the massive expansion of the skull, requiring the patient to have an extra-large grenadier's cap, to the ultimate cause of death due to the massive vascularity of the bone and high cardiac output heart failure (figure 1).

Paget's Disease of Bone has the highest prevalence in the Northern Hemisphere, then highest in the UK and within the UK in the North West of England. Although Epidemiological surveys suggest that the disease is diminishing the pattern of prevalence established by Barker et al. remains.

A number of theories have evolved as to causation. In the past it was thought that a virus may infect bone cells and stimulate abnormal increase in cell numbers, resulting proliferation of bone resorbing cells (osteoclasts) and forming cells (osteoblast). Over activity of bone cells results in production of increased amounts of bone that is markedly disorganised in structure and very vascular. A more recent theory is that a genetic mutation exists in the sequestosome gene within Paget bone cells resulting in up regulation of bone cell activity and 40% of Paget's Disease of Bone patients can carry this mutation resulting in familial Paget's. A triggering agent such as a virus may still be required to initiate the disease but if the mutation is present there is over a 98% chance the person will have Paget's Disease of Bone in later life.

The disease is mainly asymptomatic and can be present throughout the skeleton involving any bone but has a propensity to involve the axial skeleton. Spread through long bones can take many years and, although it can cause deformity, most patients present to a physician late in the disease process when symptoms arise as a result of the bone deformity causing pain, arthritis, or a neurological problem.

Diagnosis can be confirmed by blood tests. Often this happens by chance, with a "single" elevation of Alkaline Phosphatase the classic finding. X-rays may show the presence of Paget's Disease of Bone and this is often an incidental finding. Once discovered it is important to perform a Technetium bisphosphonate bone scan to demonstrate the extent of the disease at baseline as this will become very useful in managing the patient in subsequent follow up.

The mainstay of treatment is bisphosphonate therapy. Intra Venous (IV) Zoledronate is now the preferred treatment due to greater efficacy, faster onset and the prolonged effect that can be observed after a single IV 5 mg infusion when compared to oral Risedronate. It is essential to ensure adequate calcium and vitamin D status when giving IV Zoledronate as this will improve patient response and help reduce side effects of treatment.

Studies looking at intensive use of bisphosphonates versus symptomatic therapy have failed to show any benefit of aggressive bisphosphonate use and so care is required when using repeat infusions to ensure this will be of patient benefit and not detrimental.

A new approach has been adopted in an on-going study (Zoledronate in Paget's Prevention [ZiPP]) where patients with Paget's Disease of Bone are being offered sequestosome mutation screening for themselves and family members then earlier treatment with zoledronate is being given before the disease may be obvious on screening blood test or radiological testing.

First Publication of Paget's Disease of Bone

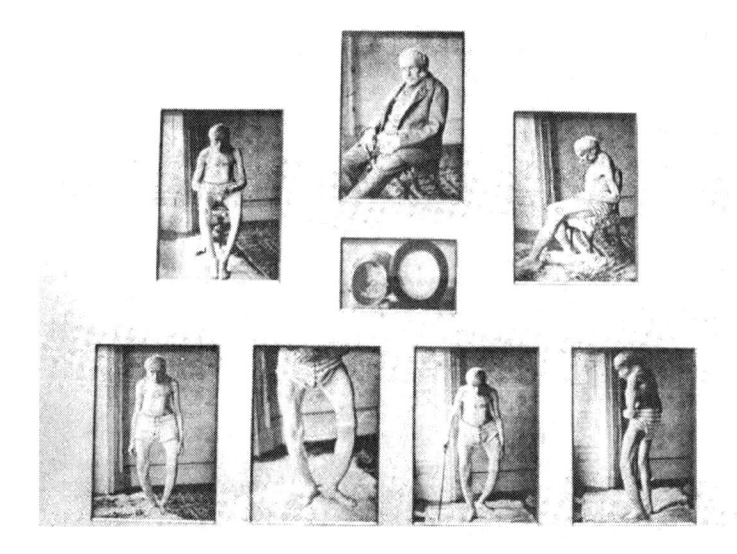

Medical Chirurgical Transactions, 1877

ORTHOPAEDIC ADVANCES

Professor Simon Donell
Honorary Professor in Musculoskeletal Surgery
Consultant Orthopaedic Surgeon
Norfolk and Norwich University Hospital
University of East Anglia

Although orthopaedic procedures, such as setting fractures, have been described in antiquity by the Egyptians and the Greeks, the term "orthopaedics" was first used by Nicholas Andry to describe straightening the child in 1741.

Orthopaedics as a speciality originates from three different professions; barber surgeons, bonesetters, and trussmakers. The bonesetters split from the barber-surgeons in 1745. "They seceded from the Mystery and Commonalty of the Barbers and Surgeons of London to become the Commonalty of the Art and Science of Surgeons of London" (A. Keith 1919). Clearly the origin of the rivalry between orthopaedic and general surgeons that exists today.

The most famous bonesetters were the Thomas' from Wales, the most famous of all being Hugh Owen Thomas (1834-1891); the father of orthopaedic surgery in Britain. In fact James Paget reported on bone setters in the very first British Medical Journal Issue "Cases that bonesetters cure", although he was denigrating their management.

Initially orthopaedics began managing club foot with William John Little (1810-1894) in London. However the advent of the First Word War put orthopaedics on the map with the work of Robert Jones (1857-1933) managing mass casualties. The simple use of a Thomas' splint to manage soldiers with femoral fractures reduced the mortality rate from 80% in 1916 to 15.7% in 1917.

Specialist orthopaedic surgeons developed after the Second World War. Many of the war hospitals became centres for managing polio and tuberculosis. These became specialist elective orthopaedic centres for joint replacement when this was developed through the 1960s and 70s. The Swiss AO School introduced dedicated fracture management tools and implants in the 1980s, and the rise of keyhole surgery at the same time reflected the improvement in the equipment and the use of Visual Display screens. Joint replacement, the management of fractures, and arthroscopic techniques are the cornerstones of orthopaedic practice today.

References:

Paget J. *Cases that bonesetters cure.* BMJ 1867; 1: 1.

Keith A. *Menders of the Maimed the Anatomical Physiological Principles Underlying the Treatment of Injuries to the Muscles, Nerves, Bones, Joints.* 1919 Reprint. Hong Kong; Forgotten Books 2013

Bentley G, Donell ST. *Orthopaedics.* In, Oxford Medical Companion. Ed Walton J, Barondess J, & Lock S, 1994.

Sir James Paget as a Family Man
Lieutenant Colonel Sir Julian Paget, Bt, CVO
Great Grandson of Sir James and the 4th Baronet

James Paget was very much a family man and, like most things in his life, he took his family responsibilities very seriously.

His childhood home was The House on the Quay in Great Yarmouth, and he spent his early years there with five brothers and two sisters. There was plenty of mental stimulus, with his father being a prosperous business man and his brothers studying various subjects. James developed an interest in botany, and together with his brother, Charles, actually wrote an authoritative book about the botany of Yarmouth - an early example of his mental and literary qualities.

But then his father's business ran into financial trouble and the house in Yarmouth had to be sold. James and his brothers nobly took over their father's debts, and it was satisfactorily resolved.

None of the family set up a 'family home' either in London or the country, which has been a sadness for later generations. But it is not surprising when the family has always consisted primarily of men in the professions, such as the Church, medicine or the services, all of whom tend to move every three years or so.

James took a keen interest in all the members of his family, and their careers, and he tried to ensure that they followed the family motto of "Work Itself is a Pleasure". They were expected, for example, to do some serious reading every morning and every evening, and he followed their careers with a close interest. The results were encouraging; John became a Q.C., Francis was Bishop of Oxford, Luke became Bishop of Chester and Stephen followed his father into Medicine becoming a distinguished surgeon and author.

James was essentially a serious man, who took life seriously. He was devout - holding family prayers every morning. He was a home-loving man, happily married, who enjoyed having an interest in his children and their achievements. He did not travel much.

He was himself a kindly person, and was said to have made sure before he went out each day that he had several sovereigns in his pocket that he would then give to any beggar that he saw.

He did not enjoy controversy, though he would argue forcibly when required, and his papers and letters were always extremely clear and conclusive.

Above all, he believed totally in his motto "Labor Ipse Voluptas", and taught his children to do the same. What he would say of the Pagets of today is debatable!

Apart from the mental qualities that Sir James bequeathed to his family, he also left two intriguing physical features. The first is the Paget probosis, a prominent, distinguished-looking nose, which has persisted through to the present generation. The other is the Paget stoop, which is highlighted by Spy in his famous cartoons, and is now evident in my stance in my 92nd year!

From Paget to The Paget - and beyond?
Willy Notcutt
Consultant in Anaesthesia and Pain Management.
Clinical Lead for Research and Development

Dr. Notcutt will look at examples of innovation at the time of Sir James Paget that radically changed the practice of medicine (eg. Introduction of Anaesthesia, the hypodermic syringe and a few others). All were totally unpredictable but revolutionary. He will then look at similar major changes which have happened over his career which have totally changed the shape of practice but including socio-political factors.

Finally he will end on pure speculation for the next 50 years.

References

Anonymous.: *"What becomes of medical students?"*. Lancet 1869, **ii:** 653-654.

Batty Shaw A. *Paget's Diseases.* Practitioner 1980 224; 1323-7

Bentley G, Donell ST. *Orthopaedics.* In, Oxford Medical Companion. Ed Walton J, Barondess J, & Lock S, 1994.

Bliss, MR. *Acute pressure area care: Sir James Paget's Legacy.* Lancet, 1992; **339:**221-223.

Breast Cancer: (early & locally advanced): diagnosis and treatment. NICE guideline CG80, February 2009.

Buchanan, WW. Rheumatology **42** issue 9 1107-1108.

Buchanan, WW. *Sir James Paget (1814–99): Surgical Osler?* Proc. R. Coll. Physicians Edinburgh 1996; **26:**91–114.

Buchanan, W. *The contribution of Sir James Paget (1814–1894) to the study of rheumatic disease.* Clin Rheumatol 1996;**15:**461–72.

Butlin, H. *On the minute Anatomy of two Breasts.* Medico-chirurgical Transaction, 1876;107.

Davies, P. *History of Medicine in Great Yarmouth Hospitals and Doctors.* 2003.

Feinstein, S. *Louise Pasteur: The Father of Microbiology.* Enslow Publishers 2008.

Godlee, R. *Lord Lister* (Second edition) Oxford University Press, 1924

Hart, I. R. & Fidler, I. J. *Role of organ selectivity in the determination of metastatic patterns of B16 melanoma.* Cancer Res. 1980; **40**:2281–2287

Hunt, A. *Plaques in and around Great Yarmouth and Gorleston.* 2013

Keith A. *Menders of the Maimed the Anatomical Physiological Principles Underlying the Treatment of Injuries to the Muscles, Nerves, Bones, Joints.* 1919 Reprint. Hong Kong; Forgotten Books 2013

Kirkes, WS. and Paget, J. *Handbook of Physiology.* 1848

Learmonth J: *The principle of decompression in the treatment of certain diseases of peripheral nerves.* Surg Clin North Am 1933;**13**:905-913

Morandi L, Pession A et al. *Intraepidermal cells of Paget's carcinoma of the breast can be genetically different from those of the underlying carcinoma.* Human Pathology, 2003; **34**, Issue 12: 1321–1330.

Marsh, H. *In Memorium.* St. Bartholomew's Hospital Reports 1900

McManus IC. *Sir James Paget's research on medical education.* Lancet 2005;**366:**506-513.

Nightingale, F. *Florence Nightingale: Extending Nursing.* Wilfrid Laurier University Press. 2009.

Oncoplastic Breast Reconstruction: Guidelines for Breast Practice. Association of Breast Surgery, November 2012

Paget, J and CJ. *Sketch of the Natural History of Yarmouth and its Neighbourhood.* 1834.

Paget, J. *Account of the Trichina spiralis.* Trans. Abernethian Society 1835.

Paget, J. *On the relation between the Symmetry and the Diseases of the Body.* Trans.Med.Chir.Soc. 1842;**25**:30.

Paget, J. *Catalogue of the Pathological Specimens in the Museum of St. Bartholomew's Hospital.* 1846.

Paget, J. *Records of Harvey, in extracts from the Journals of the Royal Hospital of St. Bartholomew.* London: John Churchill, 1846.

Paget, J. A *Descriptive Catalogue of the Pathological Specimens contained in the Museum of the Royal College of Surgeons of England.* Vol. i. 1846, vol. ii. 1847, vol. iii. 1848, vols iv. and v. 1849.

Paget, J. *On the Recent Progress of Anatomy, and its influence on Surgery.* Med. Times and Gazette July 2 1851.

Paget, J. *Lectures on Surgical Pathology.* London 1853 2 vol.

Paget, J. *On the Cause of the Rhythmic Motion of the Heart.* Croonian Lecture. Proc Roy Soc. 1857

Paget, J. *The Chronometry of Life.* Lecture at the Royal Institution. Med. Times and Gazette. 1859.

Paget, J. *On the treatment of patients after surgical operations.* Med. Times and Gazette. 1859.

Paget, J. Turner, W. *Lectures on Surgical Pathology.* Second edition. 1863.

Paget J. *Cases that bonesetters cure.* BMJ 1867; **2**:1.

Paget, J. *On Residual Abscesses* St. Bartholomew's Reports, London, 1869;**5**:73-79.

Paget, J. *What becomes of medical students?* St. Bartholomew's Hospital Reports, 1869;**5**:238-242.

Paget, J. and Turner, W. *Lectures on Surgical Pathology.* Third Edition. London: Longmans, Green and Co., 1870.

Paget, J. *Dissection Poisons.* Lancet, 10 June 1871. 775.

Paget, J. *On diseases of the Mammary Areola Preceding Cancer of the Mammary Gland.* St. Bartholomew's Hospital Reports 1874;**10**:87-90.

Paget, J, Marsh, H. *Clinical Lectures and Essays.* Longmans. 1875

Paget, J. *On a form of chronic inflammation of bones (osteitis deformans).* Trans Med Chir Soc. 1877;**60**:37–40.

Paget, J. *The Hunterian Oration of 1877.* London: Longmans, Green and Co, 1877.

Paget, J. *Additional cases of osteitis deformans, notes on seven cases.* Trans Med Chir Soc 1882;**65**:225–36.

Paget, J. *On Rare and New diseases: The Bradshaw Lecture at the College of Surgeons.* BMJ 1882 ii.

Paget, J. Goodhart, JF. and Doran, AHG. A *Descriptive Catalogue of the Pathological Specimens contained in the Museum of the Royal College of Surgeons of England.* Second Edition. 1882 -1885

Paget, J. On the utility of scientific work in practice: an introductory address at Owens College. BMJ 1887; ii.

Paget, J. *Louis Pasteur.* Nature, 26 March 1891. No. 1117;**43**:481.

Paget, J. *Studies of Old Case-books*. London: Longmans, Green and Co, 1891.

Paget, J. *The Vivisection Question*. In: Selected essays and addresses. London: Longmans, Green and Co, 1902.

Paget, S. *The distribution of secondary growths in cancer of the breast*. Lancet 1889;**1**:571–573.

Paget, S. *Memoirs and letters of Sir James Paget*. London: Longmans and Co.1901.

Paget, S. *Memoirs and letters of Sir James Paget*. 7th Impression. London: Longmans and Co. 1902.

Paget, S. *John Hunter*. London: Fisher, Unwin, 1903.

Paget S. *Sir Victor Horsley*. London: Constable, 1919.

Palmer, CJ. *Perlustrations of Great Yarmouth, with Gorleston and Southtown*. Great Yarmouth: 1872.

Parish, HJ. *A History of Immunisation*. Edinburgh and London: E and S Livingstone,1965.

Pearce, JMS. Pract. Neurol. 2009 **9:**96-99.

Plarr's Lives of the Fellows of the Royal College of Surgeons of England, Vol.II, revised by Sir D'Arcy Power. Bristol 1930. 138-41.

Porter, C.B. *A Disease of the Mammary Areola Preceding Cancer of the Mammary Glands, Paget's Disease*. Boston Med Surg J 1882; **106**:412-414.

Roberts, S. *Sir James Paget. The Rise of Clinical Surgery*. Royal Society of Medicine Services Ltd. 1989.

Sturzaker, H. *James Paget University Hospital. The first 25 years.* BookPublishingWorld 2007

Turner, W. Edinburgh Medical Journal November 1901

Wood, Richard. *Nelson's Monument, Great Yarmouth*

Index

Aberdeen Medico-Chirurgical Society, 114
Abernethian Society, 12, 44, 121, 136, 139, 148, 152, 155, 182, 188, 221
Abscesses, 21, 185, 222
Académie de Médicine, 122
Académie des Sciences, 12, 118
Académie Royale de Médecine de Belgique, 114
Academy of Medicine of New York, 95
Academy of Surgery of Philadelphia, 113
Accident and Emergency Department, 127, 177
Acle, 38
Adam Young, 78, 92
Alban Doran, 119
Albert Hall, 117
Alexander Monro, 157
Alfred Tolver Paget, 33
American Academy of Arts and Sciences, 109
Anatomy, 10, 42, 43, 47, 50, 54, 55, 56, 58, 59, 63, 64, 69, 83, 98, 146, 182, 184, 198, 208, 219, 221
Ancona, 15
Angel Inn, 38, 146
Anglo-Russian Hospital, 168
Ann Stansfield, 180
Anna Sewell, 100
Annette Tovell, 6
Apprenticeship, 10
Archbishop of York, 100, 112
Army Medical School, 120
Army Medical Service, 81
Arris and Gale Lectures, 63, 184
Arthur Coyte Paget, 30
Assistant Surgeon, 10, 58, 65, 66, 81
Association for the Advancement of Medicine by Research, 101, 163

Association of Breast Surgery, 190, 192, 193, 220
Austria, 121
Avignon, 115
Baden Baden, 86
Ballater, 86
Balmoral, 86
Barclays, 26
Basil Mayhew, 168
Battle of Camperdown, 22
Battle of Copenhagen, 16, 22
Battle of Trafalgar, 17
Bayntin, 42
Bedford Row, 53
Beer, 23
Belgium, 95
Berlin, 118, 125, 130
Bermuda, 176
Berne, 125
Bertie Howarth, 168
Biographical Dictionary, 54
Bishop of Chester, 167, 217
Bishop of London, 112
Bishop of Norwich, 8, 14, 174
Bishop of Oxford, 141, 143, 145, 164, 165, 166, 168, 217
Bishop of Stepney, 143, 167
Black Beauty, 100
Black Death, 19
Black Friars, 17
Bleeding, 52
Bloxam, 89
Bordeaux, 15
Botany, 27, 38, 43, 88
Bradshawe Lecture, 12, 115, 187
Bradwell, 24
Breast Cancer, 193, 219
Breast Care Unit, 174
Breast Screening Service, 178
Bridewell, 21
Bridge, 141
Brightwen, 28
Bristol, 19, 68, 223
Britannia, 17

British Association of Plastic, Reconstructive and Aesthetic Surgeons, 192
British Medical Association, 11, 32, 64, 82, 89, 95, 111, 114, 115, 181, 187
British Medical Benevolent Fund, 140
British Museum, 44, 48, 57, 63, 136, 148, 208
British Temperance Association, 123
Brixton, 122
Bubbles, 91
Bude, 139
Burgh Castle, 14, 24, 34, 130, 138
Burnham Thorpe, 17
Burrage Centre, 178
Busk, 74
C.E. Paget, 122
Caister, 14, 24, 34, 95
Callender, 86, 187, 199
Cambridge, 9, 12, 26, 30, 31, 41, 43, 59, 60, 95, 111, 115, 121, 142, 150, 164, 170, 174, 208
Cambridge University, 9, 121
Canterbury, 115
Captain Lacon, 17
Captain Sir Eaton Travers, 36
Cardinal Archbishop of Westminster,, 112
Care Quality Commission (CQC), 176
Caring for others, 169
Carl Linnaeus, 95
Carl Schlatter, 158
Carmelites, 17
Carole Reeve, 6
Caroline Elizabeth Paget, 33
Carpal Tunnel Syndrome, 159
Cases of Branchial Fistulae, 109, 186
Castle, 130
Catherine Paget, 164
Cavendish Laboratory, 95
Cavendish Square, 10, 71, 73
Cenrick, 14
Cerdic, 14

Charles Darwin, 81, 111
Charles Dickens, 100
Charles Hastings, 114
Charles I, 20
Charles John Paget, 32
Charlotte Street, 42
Charterhouse School, 13, 30, 35
Chemistry, 43
Chief Executive, 7, 176, 177
Chris McManus, 198
Christ Church, 60, 165, 167
Christ Church Mission, 167
Christine Allen, 7, 177
Christine Thompson, 7
Chronometry of Life, 11, 81, 131, 184, 221
Claire Rooney, 177
Clara Fardell, 32
Claude Bernard, 88
Clement John Carnell, 200
Clerical, Medical and General Life Assurance Society, 139
Clinical Lectures and Essays, 11, 101, 161, 162, 222
Clinical Society of London, 11, 86
Club of Nobody's Friends, 79
Cocklewater, 14
Collective Investigation of Diseases, 115
College of Physicians of Philadelphia, 95
Collegiate System, 59
Colonel Wodehouse, 17
Confession Medici, 168
Conge, 23
Conjoint Examinations, 98, 113
Conservative, 170
Conservator, 48, 56
Consulting Surgeon, 11, 56, 91
Copenhagen, 118
Cornwall, 53, 117, 132
Cornwall Terrace, 53
Corporation of Yarmouth, 66
Corton, 14, 24, 130, 174
Crayford, 115
Crimea, 133, 153
Critical Care Score, 178

Crocker, 156
Cromer, 131
Croonian Lecture, 10, 76, 81, 184, 221
Crown Prince of Germany, 112
Cruelty to Animals Act, 100
Crystal Palace, 113
CT Scanner, 174
Cullalloe, 17
Cuxhaven, 16
Daniel Defoe, 20
David Crossman, 7, 202
David Hill, 175, 176
David Owen, 127
David Wright, 7, 177
Dawson Turner, 23, 26, 28, 38, 44, 49, 75, 143, 146
Dean Church, 108
Dean of Norwich, 26, 126
Dean of Norwich Cathedral, 26
Dean of the Medical School, 179, 202
Dean Stanley, 107
Demonstratorship of Morbid Anatomy, 10, 55
Denes, 17
Denmark, 118
Derek Rogers, 6
Deutsche Gesellschaft fur Chirurgie, 118
Devon, 117
Dick Rainsbury, 7, 190
Director of Nursing, 177
Director of Patient Flow, 177
Disease of Mammary Areola, 5
Dispensary, 22, 56
Dissolution of the Monasteries, 21
District General Hospital, 127, 174
District Health Authority, 127, 174, 178
Dominicans, 17
Dr. Charles Costerton, 22
Dr. David Wayne, 174
Dr. Goodhart, 119, 187
Dr. Haughton, 86
Dr. Henry Monro, 62

Dr. Hue, 43
Dr. Parkes, 74
Dr. Pye-Smith, 116
Dr. William Travers Cox, 49
Dresden, 118
Duchess of Kent, 54
Duke of Argyle, 107
Duke of Cambridge, 94
Duke of Westminster, 107, 123
Duke of York, 53, 169
Duke Street, 59
Dulwich, 140
Dutch, 22, 23, 53
Dutchman, 15
E.L. LaFargue, 200
Earl of Shaftesbury, 100
Earl St. Vincent, 26
East Anglia, 23, 174, 175, 177, 179, 191, 202, 203, 204, 212, 215
East India Company, 10, 74, 75
East India Dock Road, 167
Edinburgh Medical Journal, 64, 224
Edinburgh University, 48, 64, 65
Education, 149, 197, 198, 203
Edward III, 15, 19
Edward Jenner, 127
Edward Stanley, 56, 67
Edward Stephen Paget, 33
Edward the Confessor, 14, 19
Eighth International Medical Congress, 118
Eleanor Mary Burd, 168
Elemental Pathology, 12, 111, 187
Elizabeth Blackwell, 68, 199
Elizabeth Dibden, 166
Elizabeth Sarah Paget, 30
Elma Hoare, 167
Emile Roux, 122
Endoscopic Unit, 174
England, 6, 8, 10, 11, 15, 20, 21, 38, 53, 69, 97, 99, 112, 114, 133, 139, 146, 192, 198, 199, 212, 221, 222, 223
English Heritage, 16

Epidemiological Society of London, 101
Epsom College, 140
Ernest Hart, 79
Eruder Saumier, 166
Europe, 15, 16, 19, 20, 69, 75, 125, 134, 149, 151, 171
Extramammary Paget's Disease, 156
F.W. Brown, 200
Fife, 17
Finchley Cemetery, 141
Finsbury Dispensary, 10, 55, 56
First Royal Commission on Vivisection, 100
Florence, 5, 86, 121, 133, 134, 135, 153, 171, 220
Florence Nightingale, 5, 121, 133, 134, 135, 153, 171, 220
France, 18, 53, 115, 123
Frances Alexandra Hamilton Fraser, 164
Frances Power Cope, 99, 100
Francis Paget, 32, 164, 165
Francis Turner, 26
Frankfurt, 84
Franz Konig, 158
Frederick David Stewart Sandiman, 164
Frederick Paget, 30
French, 16, 23, 28, 40, 43, 53, 122, 129, 130, 146, 149, 153, 170
General Medical Council, 9, 11, 32, 64, 103, 104, 113, 114, 133, 171
General Pathology, 63
Genetic Influences, 142
Geneva, 68
Geneva College, 68
Genoa, 15
George Eliot, 170, 201
George Paget, 5, 9, 31, 143
George Richmond, 5, 85, 171
George Taylor, 200
Georgian town, 23
German, 14, 43, 53, 130, 149, 170
German bombers, 14

Germany, 84, 118, 121
Glasgow University, 38, 89
Gonville and Caius College, 31
Gorleston, 16, 24, 34, 95, 127, 174, 220, 223
Government Schools of Art and Navigation, 66
Grand Rounds, 180
Great Exhibition, 69
Great Yarmouth, 4, 6, 8, 9, 10, 12, 13, 14, 16, 23, 32, 49, 50, 52, 94, 97, 100, 127, 142, 143, 144, 146, 148, 174, 190, 203, 208, 217, 219, 220, 223, 224
Great Yarmouth Minster, 8
Great Yarmouth Town Hall, 8
Greek, 84
Grindelwald, 125
Guinness World Record, 174
Hall Quay, 23, 26
Hamburg, 118
Hampshire, 132, 190
Hanover Square, 10, 77
Hard work, 145
Harewood Place, 10, 77, 112, 117
Harold Ellis, 7, 208
Harvey, 61, 183, 221
Hatton Garden, 50
Haven Bridge, 16
Hawarden, 170
Helen Church, 165
Henrietta Street, 10, 71, 73, 77
Henry Butlin, 97, 107, 155, 210
Henry III, 17, 19
Henry Luke Paget, 166
Henry Thomas Paget, 30
Henry Thompson, 79, 164
Henry VI, 20
Herceptin, 206
Historia Fucorum, 28
Holland, 14, 95
Holmes Coote, 11, 83
Hong Kong, 123, 216, 220
Honorary Life Governor, 56
Hospital for Sick and Wounded, 16
Hospitals, 6, 42, 113, 134, 219
House of Charity, 62, 170

House of St. Barnabas-in-Soho., 62
Hugh Owen Thomas, 215
Hugh Sturzaker, 1, 2, 189
Hunterian Professor, 48
Huxley, 107, 112, 170
Ignaz Semmelweiss, 87
Inflammation, 63, 183
Innsbruck, 124
Intensive Care Ward, 175
International Health Exhibition, 117
International Juries, 117
Ipswich Hospital, 174
Ireland, 49, 118, 122, 124
Iron Acton, 109
Islington, 122
Istanbul, 128
Italian, 53, 125, 149, 170
Jakob Kolletschka, 87
James Bentley, 59
James Clark, 53
James Paget, 1, 4, 5, 6, 7, 8, 10, 13, 20, 23, 32, 36, 48, 56, 59, 61, 65, 66, 69, 85, 93, 94, 103, 111, 113, 119, 121, 123, 126, 127, 132, 133, 134, 142, 168, 169, 173, 174, 175, 176, 179, 180, 182, 183, 189, 190, 191, 192, 193, 194, 198, 202, 203, 204, 206, 208, 209, 212, 215, 216, 219, 220, 223, 224
James Paget University Hospital, 5, 6, 7, 8, 94, 173, 175, 176, 179, 180, 189, 191, 192, 193, 194, 203, 224
James Phipps, 128
James Richard Hancorn, 200
James Sowerby, 27
James Syme, 88
James Turner, 26
James Young Simpson, 65
Jean Holden-Ross, 166
Jerome Pereira, 7, 178, 179, 191, 203
John Bell, 22
John Berney Crome, 143
John Chrome, 29, 40

John Churchill, 183, 221
John Coakley Lettsom, 95
John Everett Millais, 79, 91
John Forbes, 53
John Hemming, 176
John Hunter, 42, 56, 67, 77, 99, 123, 128, 148, 168, 223
John Major, 178
John Rahere Paget, 164
John Studley, 177
John Wells, 175
Johnstone, 42, 55
Jonathan Hutchinson, 128, 199
Joseph Eld, 200
Joseph Lister, 88, 100
Joseph Meister, 123
Joseph Solomon, 79, 80
Joshua Fitch, 117
Julia Moke, 164
Julian Paget, 165
Karen Flores, 7, 193
Katherine Paget, 33
Kenneth Churchill, 164
Kew, 38, 74, 111, 140
Kiew, 118
King John, 19
King Street, 28
Kirstead, 33, 76
La Maternite, 69
Lancashire, 58
Lancet, 89, 90, 168, 185, 186, 198, 202, 219, 220, 222, 223
Langenbeck, 112
Latin, 84
Law of Banking, 164
Learmonth, 160, 220
Leatherhead, 117
Lecturer in Physiology, 10, 11, 58, 81
Lectures in Surgical Pathology, 10, 63, 149, 160
Leeches, 21
Leeds Clergy School, 167
Leeds School of Medicine, 83, 185
Leo, 86
Lesley Fallowfield, 193
Liberal, 62, 170

226

Lily Burrage, 178
Limpsfield, 168
Linnean Society, 11, 95
Lithotomy, 66
Liverpool, 32, 60, 115
Liz Libiszewski, 177
London, 8, 11, 12, 13, 17, 19, 21, 22, 26, 35, 36, 37, 41, 42, 52, 53, 60, 64, 66, 73, 80, 81, 83, 85, 89, 91, 100, 103, 104, 108, 110, 111, 112, 114, 116, 118, 125, 128, 132, 134, 137, 139, 141, 157, 160, 167, 170, 171, 181, 183, 185, 186, 187, 188, 198, 199, 202, 203, 208, 215, 217, 221, 222, 223
London University, 8, 11, 12, 81, 116, 125, 132, 188
Lord Acton, 107
Lord Aldenham, 79
Lord Duncan, 26
Lord Herschell, 127, 128
Lord Nelson, 16, 26
Lord Palmerston, 170
Lord Rectorship of Aberdeen University, 113
Louis Pasteur, 88, 129, 139, 223
Lowestoft, 127, 130, 174
Lucerne, 124
Lutyens Suite, 181
Lydia North, 10, 52, 59
Lying-in Institutions, 134
Madeleine Borg, 6
Manchester, 124, 180
Mansion House, 129, 188
Margate, 132
Maria Ann Paget, 32
Mark Rumble, 28
Mark Wilkinson, 7, 204
Market Place, 16, 18, 21, 22, 38
Marseilles, 20
Martha Maud Paget, 30
Mary Lloyd, 100
Massachusetts Medical Society, 114
Mastership in Oncoplastic Breast Surgery, 204
Mayor of Yarmouth, 26

Medical Act of 1858, 104
Medical care, 21
Medical Director, 177
Medical Gazette, 53, 199, 209
Medical Jurisprudence, 50
Medical School, 42, 68, 72, 133, 157, 175, 202, 203, 208, 212
Medical Society of Constantinople, 129
Medical Society of London, 95, 101, 113
Medicine, 6, 32, 42, 43, 48, 50, 53, 61, 65, 87, 101, 114, 116, 118, 124, 133, 167, 183, 208, 212, 217, 219, 224
Medico-Chirurgical Society, 11, 53, 75, 101, 104, 114, 156, 171
Medico-Chirurgical Society of Edinburgh, 75
Memoirs and Letters of Sir James Paget, 6, 168
Metropolitan Hospital, 167
Michael Thompson, 139
Microbiology, 219
Microscope, 182
Middlemarch, 201
Middlesex Hospital, 167
Midwifery, 43, 65, 193
Mike Pollard, 175
Millman Street, 53
Monitor, 177
Moscow, 118
Motives to Industry, 61, 183
Mr. Bowles, 5, 32, 34, 35, 146
Mr. Children, 44
Mr. Cooper, 130
Mr. Eve, 119
Mr. Fairbank, 78
Mr. Hilton, 160
Mr. Kerridge, 25
Mr. Lawrence, 43
Mr. McWhinnie, 65
Mr. Palgrave, 38
Mr. Randall, 38
Mr. Swann, 160
Mr. Syme, 86
MRI Scanner, 175

Mrs. Godfrey, 28
Mrs. Scharlieb, 110
Mrs. Suckling, 17
Munich, 85
Museum, 5, 6, 10, 12, 42, 54, 55, 56, 61, 67, 68, 119, 123, 133, 160, 182, 188, 209, 221, 222
Music in Villages, 169
Naples, 15, 16
Napoleon, 27
National Anti-Vivisection Society, 100
National Gold Award, 179
National Health Service, 21, 179
National Institute for Health and Care Excellence (NICE), 192
National Mastectomy and Breast Reconstruction Audit, 191
National Portrait Gallery, 94
Natural History Department, 44, 48
Natural History Museum, 48
Natural Selection of Species, 115
Nature, 22, 84, 130, 188, 223
Nelson Arms, 17
Nelson Hotel, 17
Netley Hospital, 120, 187
New York, 68, 69, 181, 199
New York State, 68
NHS Trust, 175, 192
Nice, 114
Nicholas Andry, 215
Nick Oligbo, 177
Nightingale School of Nursing, 133
Nobel Prize, 143
Noel Johnson, 178
Norfolk and Norwich Hospital, 22
North Sea, 14, 26, 138
North Wales, 81, 84
Northgate, 21, 127
Northgate Hospital, 22, 127
Northgate Street, 21
Norway, 23
Norwich, 11, 20, 22, 29, 38, 50, 60, 95, 180, 202, 204, 212, 215
Nurse Finn, 139

Nutrition, 63, 183
Odontological Society of Great Britain, 107
Ontario, 69
Ophelia, 91
Order of Merit, 89
Osgood-Schlatter disease, 158
Osteitis Deformans, 156
Osteitis Dessicans, 157
Oulton Broad, 130
Owens College, 124, 188, 222
Oxford Medical Society, 132
Oxford Street, 77
Oxford University, 86, 165, 219
Paget and Company, 27
Paget as a man, 173
Paget Bicentenary Conference, 4, 7
Paget cells, 97, 206
Paget Club, 180
Paget Foundation, 181
Paget Recurrent Fibroid Tumours, 161
Paget Residual Abscesses, 162
Paget-Schroetter Disease, 161
Pain Relief Clinic, 177
Palliative Care Unit, 175
Paris, 53, 69, 75, 123, 125, 139, 162
Park Square West, 12, 136, 139
Parliament, 20, 115, 170
Pasteur Committee, 12, 122, 162
Pathological Catalogue, 10, 12, 55, 67, 112, 119, 182
Pathological Society of London, 12, 101, 124, 188
Paul Davies, 6, 35, 51
Pembroke College, Oxford, 49
Pembroke Hall, 26
Penny Cyclopaedia, 54
Percivall Pott, 42
Periostitis, 158
Peter Franzen, 176
Peter Mere Latham, 49
Peter Ransome, 7
Petrograd, 168
Philosophical Club, 81

Philosophical Society of
  Cambridge, 75
Philosophical Society of
  Philadelphia, 74
Physics, 43, 143
Physiological Society, 64, 114
Physiology, 10, 43, 50, 58, 64, 72,
  73, 74, 98, 100, 149, 182, 183,
  184, 198, 220
Pinner, 76
Plague, 19
Plaster of Paris, 152
Poorhouse, 21
Poplar, 167
Practice of Medicine, 151
Press gangs, 19
Prince Charles, 174
Prince of Orange, 20
Prince of Wales, 8, 82, 86, 91, 95,
  107, 112, 117, 126, 169, 209
Prince William, 174
Princess Diana, 174
Princess of Wales, 73, 84, 86
Progress of Anatomy and
  Physiology, 53
Provincial Medical and Surgical
  Association, 114
Public Speaking, 172
Pudding Gate, 21
Purcell, 86
Putnam, 160
Pyrenees, 123
Quarterly Review, 53, 58, 184
Queen Street, 22
Queen Victoria, 8, 54, 77, 78, 80,
  100, 108, 126, 169, 180, 209
Rabies, 162
Rahere, 5, 41, 48, 164, 165
Rare and New Diseases, 12, 115
Reale Accademia di Medicina di
  Roma, 113
Registration of Nurses, 133
Regius Professor of Physic, 9, 32,
  111, 142
Research Defence Society, 167
Retinal Screening Programme,
  177
Reverend Henry North, 53

Rhine, 84
Rhythmic Motion of the Heart,
  10, 76, 221
Richard II, 19
Richard Owen, 47, 56, 155
Richmond, 111, 140
Risks of Operations, 185
Robert Bayley Osgood, 158
Robert Brown, 44, 49, 100
Robert Browning, 100
Robin Hood's Bay, 130
Rokitansky, 75, 170
Roman Catholic Church, 60
Romans, 14
Rome, 125, 130
Roundell Palmer, 62
Royal Academy, 80, 112
Royal and Religious Foundation
  of St. Katharine's, 124
Royal College of Physicians, 32,
  76, 99, 101, 104
Royal College of Surgeons, 6, 7,
  8, 10, 11, 12, 38, 46, 47, 48,
  49, 50, 51, 56, 68, 69, 72, 83,
  97, 99, 103, 105, 112, 119,
  122, 128, 139, 146, 148, 163,
  180, 192, 198, 199, 210, 221,
  222, 223
Royal Commission on
  Vaccination, 12, 127, 128, 163
Royal Institution, 11, 74, 81, 112,
  184, 221
Royal Medical Society of
  Edinburgh, 65
Royal Medico-Chirurgical
  Society, 101
Royal Navy, 26, 36, 75, 143, 146,
  164
Royal Sanitary Commission, 86
Royal Society, 8, 9, 10, 32, 48,
  51, 62, 64, 69, 76, 95, 101,
  112, 114, 133, 171, 224
Royal Society of Edinburgh, 95
Royal Society of Sciences of
  Upsala, 114
Royalty, 19, 169
Runcorn, 115
Russia, 15, 23, 118

Sam Leinster, 179
Samuel Paget, 5, 23, 24, 25, 26, 27, 28, 30, 36, 38, 50, 66, 67, 142
San Martino, 124, 125
Sandra Chapman, 174, 178
Sandringham, 95
Sanitation, 19
Sarah Elizabeth Tolver, 28
Saxons, 14
Schaffhausen, 125
School of Practical Geology, 112
School of Science and Art, 66
Science, 147, 187, 215
Scientific Study in the Practice of Medicine and Surgery, 131
Scotland, 17, 86, 108
Sergeant Surgeon, 78, 108
Serle Street, 55, 59
Seven Ages of Man, 138
Shakespeare, 138
Sheffield, 83
Shipping Clubs of Yarmouth, 67
Shirley Roberts, 6
Shoreditch, 200
Shrewsbury, 33, 76, 165, 167
Sidestrand, 131
Simon Donell, 7, 215
Sir Astley Cooper, 5, 50, 51, 67, 97, 130
Sir Bernard Charles Tolver Paget, 143
Sir Charles Locock, 86
Sir Edgar Boehm, 5, 118, 119, 171
Sir Edmund Lacon, 27
Sir Edward Fry, 116
Sir Edwin Lutyens, 181
Sir George Humphrey, 32
Sir Henry Acland, 132, 133, 139
Sir Henry Thompson, 79, 140
Sir Hermann Weber, 140
Sir Hyde Parker, 16
Sir J. Russell Reynolds, 133
Sir James Paget Library, 7, 178, 180
Sir James Paget Room, 181
Sir James Smith, 27
Sir John Simon, 86
Sir Joseph John Thomson, 143
Sir Julian Paget, 5, 6, 7, 25, 27, 29, 31, 166, 216
Sir Risdon Bennett, 112
Sir Rutherford Alcock, 123
Sir Samuel Wilks, 140, 209
Sir Thomas Smith, 86, 171, 199
Sir William Gull, 86, 101, 112, 171
Sir William Hamilton, 16
Sir William Hooker, 38, 146
Sir William Priestley, 140
Sir William Turner, 64, 82, 83, 87
Sketch of the Natural History, 10, 39, 182, 220
Smallpox, 123, 128, 163
Smithfield, 41
Société de Chirurgie, 82
Society for the Relief of Widows and Orphans of Medical Men, 140
South Kensington Museum, 112
South Quay, 5, 13, 14, 20, 23, 24, 32, 33, 34, 60, 75, 85, 132
Spaniards, 23
Spy, 5, 11, 102, 103, 218
St. Bartholomew's, 4, 5, 7, 10, 11, 12, 32, 37, 40, 41, 42, 47, 48, 50, 53, 54, 56, 57, 58, 59, 61, 63, 64, 65, 67, 69, 73, 81, 83, 86, 89, 91, 93, 94, 95, 107, 110, 113, 120, 121, 133, 139, 140, 146, 148, 149, 155, 161, 164, 167, 180, 182, 183, 185, 187, 198, 203, 220, 221, 222
St. Bartholomew's Hospital, 4, 7, 10, 37, 41, 42, 48, 57, 61, 86, 91, 93, 94, 95, 113, 120, 121, 139, 155, 161, 180, 182, 183, 187, 198, 220, 221, 222
St. Bartholomew's Hospital Reports, 86, 95, 155, 161, 220, 222
St. Bennet's Church, 14
St. Dominica, 17
St. George's Chapel, 23, 144
St. George's Hospital, 59

St. Ives, 123
St. Mary's, 21, 60, 109, 123
St. Mary's Hall, 123
St. Nicholas Church, 17, 20, 24, 126, 132, 144
St. Nicholas Road, 22
St. Pancras, 167
St. Petersburgh, 118
St. Thomas' Hospital, 133, 141
Stanley, 42, 43, 81
Stephen Paget, 112, 167, 169, 202
Studies of Old Case-Books, 12, 122, 158
Sue Down, 7, 191
Surgeon Extraordinary, 1, 10, 54, 80, 108
Surgery, 6, 10, 11, 22, 32, 43, 52, 63, 69, 79, 83, 88, 89, 95, 108, 116, 127, 133, 153, 179, 184, 185, 186, 208, 215, 221, 224
Sweden, 23
Syphilis, 186
Tenerife, 16
Tenth International Medical Congress, 125
Tercentenary Festival of Dublin University, 132
Tercentenary Festival of Edinburgh University, 118
Terry Mitchell, 174
Thavies Inn, 42, 50
The Boyhood of Raleigh, 91
The Fight against Disease, 167
Thomas Fastolph, 21
Thomas Oldham Barlow, 93
Times, 63, 98, 129, 183, 184, 185, 221
Tina Cookson, 177
Tom Oliver Hunt, 200
Tom Tolver, 28
Tommy Wormald, 43, 47, 155
Tory MP, 62
Tory party, 29
Trichina spiralis, 5, 10, 43, 47, 57, 136, 154, 155, 221
Trieste, 15
Trinity College, Dublin, 49, 124
Tumours, 63, 184

Typhoid Fever, 186
University College Hospital, 79
University College, Liverpool, 130, 188
University College, London, 88
University of Bonn, 86
University of Pest, 88
University of Wursburg, 114
Upton, 88
Vaccination, 127, 163
Vanity Fair, 11, 102
Venice, 15, 86
Verily Anderson, 167
Verona, 124
Victor Horsley, 123, 168, 188, 223
Victoria Hotel, 125, 132
Victoria Street Society, 100
Vienna Lying-in Hospital, 88
Virchow Testimonial Fund, 12, 130
Virgin Mary, 21
Vivisection, 99, 101, 163, 187, 223
Volunteer Corps, 26
Wales, 11, 132, 133, 136, 139, 140, 192, 215
Warsaw, 118
Weiner, 156
Wellcome Trust, 7
Wendy Slaney, 176
West London Hospital, 167
Westminster Abbey, 12, 141
What becomes of Medical Students, 11, 86, 185
Whitefriars, 17
Wiesbaden, 84
Wildbad, 86
Wilkie Collins, 80
William Clift, 48, 56
William Croone, 76
William Fergusson, 78, 108
William Holden Hunt, 91
William III, 20
William Jenner, 86, 112, 124
William MacCormac, 113
William Osler, 198
William Palmer, 199

William Pennington, 65
William Pitt, 26
Wimbledon, 124
Wimpole Street, 79
Wood, 224
Worcester, 114
Worcester Infirmary, 114
World Health Organisation, 128, 163
Writing, 173
Yarmouth, 5, 6, 13, 14, 15, 16, 17, 18, 19, 20, 21, 22, 23, 26, 27, 28, 30, 36, 37, 38, 39, 44, 49, 53, 60, 66, 75, 76, 81, 94, 95, 111, 125, 126, 127, 130, 132, 136, 138, 174, 182, 208, 210, 217, 220, 223
Yarmouth Corporation, 22
Yarmouth General Hospital, 5, 49, 94, 127, 174
Yarmouth Troll Cart, 19
York, 19, 69
Zoledronate, 213, 214
Zoological Society, 47, 155

Lightning Source UK Ltd.
Milton Keynes UK
UKOW04f1647181213

223272UK00002B/2/P